Rhetoric of the Asia Higher Education Rankings

Rhetoric of the Asia Higher Education Rankings

By

Kolawole Samuel Adeyemo

BRILL

LEIDEN | BOSTON

Cover illustration: iStock.com/fcscafeine

All chapters in this book have undergone peer review

Library of Congress Cataloging-in-Publication Data

Names: Adeyemo, Kolawole Samuel, author.
Title: Rhetoric of the Asia higher education rankings / By Kolawole Samuel Adeyemo.
Description: Leiden ; Boston : Brill, [2023] | Includes bibliographical references and index.
Identifiers: LCCN 2022058791 (print) | LCCN 2022058792 (ebook) | ISBN 9789004543362 (hardback) | ISBN 9789004543355 (paperback) | ISBN 9789004543379 (ebook)
Subjects: LCSH: Universities and colleges--Ratings and rankings--Asia. | Education, Higher--Social aspects--Asia. | Higher education and state--Asia. | Educational equalization--Asia.
Classification: LCC LB2331.65.A78 A34 2023 (print) | LCC LB2331.65.A78 (ebook) | DDC 378.5--dc23/eng/20221214
LC record available at https://lccn.loc.gov/2022058791
LC ebook record available at https://lccn.loc.gov/2022058792

Typeface for the Latin, Greek, and Cyrillic scripts: "Brill". See and download: brill.com/brill-typeface.

ISBN 978-90-04-54335-5 (paperback)
ISBN 978-90-04-54336-2 (hardback)
ISBN 978-90-04-54337-9 (e-book)

Copyright 2023 by Koninklijke Brill NV, Leiden, The Netherlands.
Koninklijke Brill NV incorporates the imprints Brill, Brill Nijhoff, Brill Hotei, Brill Schöningh, Brill Fink, Brill mentis, Vandenhoeck & Ruprecht, Böhlau, V&R unipress and Wageningen Academic.
All rights reserved. No part of this publication may be reproduced, translated, stored in a retrieval system, or transmitted in any form or by any means, electronic, mechanical, photocopying, recording or otherwise, without prior written permission from the publisher. Requests for re-use and/or translations must be addressed to Koninklijke Brill NV via brill.com or copyright.com.

This book is printed on acid-free paper and produced in a sustainable manner.

Contents

Foreword VII
   Amy Verdun
Acknowledgements VIII
List of Figures and Tables IX

Introduction 1

1 **A Rhetorical Analysis of Reputation Rankings** 5
  1 Introduction 5
  2 Debriefing Rankings 8
  3 Rephrasing Misconceptions in Rankings 11
  4 Analysis of QS Reputation Rankings in Asia 14

2 **QS World University Rankings' Metrics Analysis** 28
  1 Introduction 28
  2 Modelling and Analysis of QS Ranking Methodologies 29
  3 Academic Reputation 35
  4 Employer Reputation 36
  5 Faculty/Student Ratio 39
  6 Citations per Faculty 42
  7 International Faculty/International Student Ratio 43
  8 Conclusion 47

3 **Critiquing Ranking Methods** 50
  1 Introduction 50
  2 Purpose and Methodology of Rankings in Asia 54
  3 Concluding Thoughts 59

4 **Theorizing 'Comparison' in Ranking Systems** 64
  1 Introduction 64
  2 Ranking and National Identity 65
  3 Power and Politics in Rankings 67
  4 Responding to Social Issues 69

5   **Aligning Rankings to Cultural and Social Identities**   74
    1   Introduction   74
    2   Results of Ranking in Asian Higher Education   75
    3   Evaluating Social Importance in Asia   79
    4   Concluding Thoughts   82

Appendix: Overall Score and Ranking Dataset   86
Index   146

Foreword

Not a day goes by, or scholars, students, and educational professionals worry about university rankings. Institutions of higher education, all across the globe, seek to improve their 'standing', whether it is on 'reputation' or 'student happiness' or 'journal citations'. What do these rankings do to the way universities are managed? How do individuals determine where they want to work or study? Across the globe, parents consider rankings when deciding what 'investment' they wish to make in the education of their children. Governments consult the rankings of their institutions of higher learning when determining the level of public spending they wish to make to support the sector. Even philanthropists consider university success (in terms of rankings) as they contemplate whom to give their money.

This book offers a much-needed critical analysis into university rankings from the perspective of the scholar from Global South. Focusing on the massive changes made in recent years to Asian institutions of higher learning, it problematizes these rankings in terms of what aspect of university life gets attention. It also offers us a look into how a focus on rankings has all kinds of unintended consequences. For instance, the best and the brightest students and scholars are drawn to the established universities with the highest rankings, thereby draining the potential from local places in the Global South in favor of the Global North. These forces ensure that many of these underlying power-relations are reinforced. The existing university landscape therefore may remain intact due to these pressures even as universities in the Global South increase in quality and in potential.

The existence of these standardized rankings poses a dilemma, however. On the one hand, they tend to reinforce those institutions that are already on top as they have an almost magnetic attraction to drawing in more of everything (better scholars, better students, more research funding and so on) thereby reinforcing the already existing hierarchy of universities. On the other hand, the very existence of these rankings means that there is a clear target that would-be excellent universities can aim for.

The challenge, of course, remains that the inequities are so profound throughout the world that one knows that universities in Asia and elsewhere the Global South have a steep climb before being able to catch up. The present book provides us food for thought to reflect on, and invites us to think about strategies to address, these inequities.

Amy Verdun
Professor of Political Science, University of Victoria, Canada
Visiting Professor, Leiden University, The Netherlands

Acknowledgements

I would like to acknowledge the following academics, students, indiviudals, and institutions for their contributions to the success of this book project.

Chika Sehoole, Professor and Education Dean at the University of Pretoria, South Africa for his critical comments on one of the chapters and support during my sabbatical at the University of Victoria in Canada.

Professors Cyril Hartell and Siphiwe Mthiyane of the Department of Education Management and Policy Studies at the University of Pretoria, South Africa for their support during my absence.

Amy Verdun, Professor of Political Science at the University of Victoria in Canada for her feedback that enriched the quality of the manuscript.

Ophielie Dangbegnon, a Ph.D. student in Education Policy at the University of Pretoria in South Africa for excellent proofreading and language editing of the whole manuscript.

Olarenwaju Adediran, a Ph.D. student in Economics at the University of Witwatersrand in South Africa for the analysis of statistics and quantitative data.

Leadership and fellows at the Centre for Studies in Religion and Society (CSRS) of the University of Victoria in Canada for hosting me and for their intellectual contributions during daily coffee talks that have shaped my writing and world views.

Management of the University of Pretoria for their great support that empowered me to complete this book.

Lastly, a special acknowledgment to my wife, Mary Margaret Adeyemo, and son, Emmanuel Ife Adeyemo for their moral support.

Also, thanks to my parents, Revered A.O. and Revered (Mrs) Deboral O. Adeyemo for their prayers and continuous support of my career.

Figures and Tables

Figures

1   Classification according to institutions' size.   31
2   The focus of institutions.   32
3   The research of institutions.   33
4   The age of institutions.   33
5   The status of institutions, whether public or private.   34
6   Criteria of most influential institution ranking bodies.   52

Tables

1   QS World University Rankings data.   14
2   Regression for institutional characteristics and citations per faculty rank.   15
3   Institutional characteristics and international faculty rank.   17
4   Regression of rank indicators on the log of the overall score.   18
5   Pairwise correlations of institutions' academic reputation.   36
6   Pairwise correlation of employment rank.   37
7   Institutional characteristics and employer reputation rank.   38
8   Pairwise correlation of faculty-student ranking.   39
9   Institutional characteristics and faculty student rank.   40
10 Institutional characteristics and International Students Rank.   41
11 Pairwise correlation of citations per faculty.   43
12 Pairwise correlation of international faculty score.   43
13 Institutional characteristics and International Faculty Rank.   45
14 Institutional characteristics and International Students Score.   46
15 Institutional characteristics and log of the overall score.   47

Introduction

Despite varying and inconstant resources, Asian higher education institutions continue to perform well in World University Rankings. Nevertheless, further analysis is required to understand the meanings of this strong performance for the future of ranking systems. Understanding the impact of ranking criteria and the associated rhetoric on social issues in Asia calls for the analysis of these factors since such an investigation has yet to be undertaken. This book analyzes the Quacquarelli Symonds (QS) World University ranking metrics and the methodology use to rank the institutions in the Asian higher education sector. The dataset is a panel of higher education institutions in the Asian region that are in the top 100. An estimation of institutions' size, focus, research, age, and status on the academic reputation ranking using the ordinary least squares (OLS) method is given in the data. Furthermore, university ranking indicators and metrics used by QS were modeled along with institutional characteristics. The overall score and ranking dataset from the QS report for 2012, 2013, 2018, 2019 and 2020 represent the data distribution used for the analysis. The results suggest several factors responsible for the misconceptions and interpretations of ranking results in Asian countries.

The results of the analysis are somewhat counter-intuitive. For instance, as academic ranking increases, institutional characteristics such as 'size' decrease. In addition, institutional characteristics such as 'status', 'size', 'focus', and 'research' increase, while institution 'age' in terms of the year of establishment decreases. These findings imply that the 'size' and 'age' of institutions alone cannot assist institutions in maintaining a culture of quality and ranking status. Meanwhile, the 'age' and 'status' of private or public institutions have increased with an increase in faculty-student ranking. Also, with a one-unit increase in 'citation' ranking, an increase in 'size' (20.2%) and 'focus' (25.8%) is noted. The increase in factors indicates that the 'size' and academic 'focus' of institutions contribute to the academic research outputs to some extent. However, institutions' 'research' and 'age' decrease with an increase in 'citation' ranking. This negative correlation reveals that the institution's age cannot sustain its research capability and productivity. Similarly, a unit increase in international faculty rank led to an increase in 'size' (20.1%), focus (2.74%), 'research' (19.16%), and 'age' (44.12%). Here, institution 'size', 'focus', and 'research' contributes to attracting international academics. However, the institutional 'status' reduces by 8.4% when international faculty rank increases, which shows that the status of institutions as private or public is not a determinant of academic mobility. Moreover, a unit increase in international students rank yields an increase in 'size' (19.7%), 'research' (23.2%), 'age' (38.72%), and 'status' (7.2%), which shows the importance of these criteria in international students mobility activity.

Asian institutions have changed their governance and quality policy to suit QS criteria to perform better in the global rankings. These efforts have generated considerable success; indeed, these days well-ranked Asian institutions have an academic focus and research activities comparable to 'elite' and 'world-class' universities in the West. The research presented in this study finds that a unit increase in the academic reputation score leads to an increase in 'size' (33.1%), 'focus' (31.8%), 'research' (7%), and 'age' (31.9%), meaning that academic reputation rankings in Asia are linked to the focus, research, and age of the institutions in this region. The changes made by universities could have an effect on national cultural identity and development, however. This book critically assesses these pressures and explores the pros and cons of these developments.

Ranking criteria are changing policies on university governance and the Asian higher education landscape. This book provides evidence of the role of ranking criteria as a factor for change in staffing, resource allocation, and research collaboration among Asian institutions. It is unlikely that weighting and metrics can affect institutions' performance in Asia. The analysis provides several criteria used in QS rankings, suggests factors responsible for the errors, and offers policy recommendations on each of the findings. The ranking methodology does not often respond strategically to the systemic issues responsible for institutions' varied ability to produce quality. This book backs up its claims with numerical evidence and highlights the impact of social inequalities on the ability to deliver quality in Asia, a crucial factor.

The literature and data analysis highlights how reputation ranking shapes cultural identity and development in Asia. The essential emphasis on academic reputation in this analysis is missing from the rankings table, despite its profound effect on policy, resource allocation, student mobility, and research collaboration. The main argument is that the rankings methodology for Asian higher education and that of developing countries need to follow a grass-roots approach to connect reputation status to social development.

Chapter 1 introduces different perspectives and a conceptualization of rankings in different contexts with a particular focus on Asia. It applies a critical approach to present the influence of varying factors and criteria on rankings' social return. The central question in Chapter 1 is whether the rankings narrative contributes to solving issues encountered in Asian higher education institutions. What's more, theoretical predictions were made based on the analysis of QS data for Asian institutions, based on some parameters of the model derived during the investigation. These predictions serve as the benchmark for comparing the QS rankings methodology analysis' results in this chapter.

Chapter 2 focuses on the academic reputation indicator of rankings among Asian higher education institutions. In this chapter, the estimation consists of the result of the various models specified in QS ranking methods and criteria. The analysis presents the estimation of size, focus, research, age, and status on the academic reputation rank using ordinary least squares (OLS). The findings reveal that the institutional characteristics have a negative relationship with the reputation rankings. The result of the analysis clearly indicates that several factors, which are ignored in the QS methodology ranking, may be responsible for the inconsistency in performance in the ranking tables for many higher education institutions in Asia and other developing countries. For the most part, the reputation factor and ranking are mainly responsible for the unequal representation of international students.

Similarly, Chapter 3 explains some quantitative methods and techniques used to understand QS rankings. The statistical approach is used to analyze the challenges concerning scores allocation and application when ranking Asian higher education institutions. The explanation describes how ranking methodologies are used to determine or make predictions for the performance of higher education institutions based on QS criteria. In this chapter, the analysis provides various advantages to contexts in assessing the weight of the performance of higher education institutions. Likewise, an account of ranking scores' fair calculations to include institutions in the Global South was given. The chapter argues that a collaborative policy with stakeholders among participating institutions was crucial for a holistic view of the metrics, weighting, and criteria used in rankings. Such a policy could prove vital as it could facilitate fairness and acknowledge the different systemic factors that could interfere with ranking results.

Chapter 4 speaks to the idea of using similar criteria in comparing profoundly different universities. The writing reframes the motivations and implications of ranking Asian universities without taking note of the systemic issues that could interfere with ranking activities in this region. Asian higher education institutions with a long history and adequate resources are likely to compete well, which is a deeply political issue as funding for higher education is mainly dependent on several political factors in many Asian countries. Despite reputation ranking, age, and status of institutions, research performance has not improved significantly in the region. One notable argument is that comparing research also depends on adequate funding. There have been instances where funding was not well allocated, distributed, or utilized to improve the quality of higher education systems. However, there is evidence that the Asian higher education institutions have improved in recent rankings, not necessarily because of the QS criteria.

Finally, Chapter 5 deals with national cultural identity in rankings in Asia. The analysis indicates an improved performance in Asian higher education rankings, but this improvement may have resulted from changes in academic activities to suit rankings criteria. It means curriculum and research may not necessarily reflect the value systems of the country, per se. While rankings have provided beneficial information about the performance of universities in Asia, it may be necessary to redefine what it entails for the region's development.

Academics, policymakers, postgraduate students, and government agencies responsible for the quality and accreditation of higher education will find the analysis in this book valuable.

CHAPTER 1

A Rhetorical Analysis of Reputation Rankings

Abstract

The narratives of globalization (Lee, 2015) and elitism of rankings (Lo & Hou, 2020) may have underscored the dominant power of Western knowledge in developing countries besides Asia. This chapter introduces different perspectives and analyzes the goals of reputation rankings in the Asian higher education systems. The analysis includes debriefing, rephrasing, and exposing how World Reputation Rankings systematically create tension in the governance of higher education. The chapter challenged the neoliberal approaches to university rankings and deconstructs the rhetoric that higher education should be ranked. Essentially, it explains how reputation rankings may be increasing social inequalities in research and internationalization in higher education.

Keywords

reputation rankings – rhetoric – higher education – globalization – Asia

1 **Introduction**

Higher education systems have experienced tremendous change and undergone national reforms and revolutions due to the forces of globalization (Altbach, Reisberg, & Rumbley, 2019). These changes took the form of massification, and intellectual competition and were informed either by egalitarian or elitist ideologies after the Second World War (see Zha, 2013, 2020; Tight, 2019). As public spending for higher education continues to decline especially in Southeast Asia (Tilak, 2015), higher education costs increase in East Asia for "quality" reasons (Hawkins, 2010), leading to an increase in the enrollment rate and increased participation of private providers of higher education (Shin & Harman, 2009) in East Asia and Pacific and South Asia (Rifa'i, Irwandi, & Mendy, 2019). As a result, higher education framed by an egalitarian ideology distributes power and wealth to the elite, which encourages world-class university reputation rankings aspirations in Asia and in East Asia, specifically (Hou, Hill, Hu, & Lin, 2022).

The pursuit of a world-class university status in ranking has been profoundly challenged for converting higher education's mission to market orientation (see Ng, 2012). The persuasive yet compelling narrative in reputation rankings is that universities that are not on ranking tables are of low quality or do not pursue excellence. This situation leads one to suggest that global ranking systems and their narratives may have intentionally created unnecessary competition among universities. Such a competition is then based on unjust principles as rankings geographically and historically favors elite universities (see Hazelkorn, 2015; Marginson & Van der Wende, 2007) to control the flow of international students (see Perkins & Neumayer, 2014), and knowledge production (see Ortega & Busch-Armendariz, 2014).

Quacquarelli Symonds (QS) World University Rankings, the Times Higher Education (THE) World University Rankings and the Academic Ranking of World Universities (ARWU) are the most popular ranking agencies and have also committed to showcasing Sustainable Development Goals (SDGs) through the evaluation and assessment of university performances (Galleli, Teles, dos Santos, Freitas-Martins, & Junior, 2021; Taylor & Braddock, 2007).

Since the introduction of the Academic Ranking of World Universities (ARWU) rankings in 2003 (Douglass, 2016), the brain race for recognition, reputation, and the move towards world-class university status has increased in Asia due to the focus on STEM (Lee, Liu, & Wu, 2020). Though the competition for world-class status and emphasis on global rankings is growing, Southeast Asia remains underdeveloped (Marginson, 2010). In 2020 and more recent global rankings, East Asian universities in China, Japan, and Korea represent Asia in the top 200 best world-class universities (Lee, Liu, & Wu, 2020). In the 2021 QS World University rankings, the best ranked higher education in the ASEAN region was the National University of Singapore, which placed eleventh (11). The other high-ranking ASEAN higher education Institutions are China's Tsinghua University and Peking University, Hong Kong's University of Science and Technology and the University of Hong Kong, and Singapore's Nanyang Technological University (NTU) (Quacquarelli Symonds [QS], 2021). The performance of these institutions can be attributed primarily to internationalization and their research capacity. After twenty-seven (27) years, ASEAN countries now embrace internationalization as a regional approach to higher education.

The first global rankings in Asian nations were the 2003 Academic Rankings of World Universities (ARWU) by the Shanghai Jiao Tong University (Hazelkorn, 2014). The ARWU rankings established international comparison rankings to compare Chinese higher education institutions to global competitors. Subsequently, other countries adopted ARWU after the report's publication in the Economist (Universities & Rankings, 2021).

In 2021, QS ranked 1,000 out of 4,700 participating institutions, THE ranked 1,250 institutions, and ARWU ranked the top 500 out of 1,200 institutions (Collier, 2021). Despite the multitude of ranking agencies in existence, this chapter analyzes reputation scores of the Quacquarelli Symonds (QS) World University rankings to unravel the narrative on reputation rankings, while explaining how rankings could determine power and politics in global higher education systems. What is often concealed in any ranking reports is the counterfactual effects of not having to rank universities. In other words, what would or could be the influence of a lack of ranking on the quality, funding, and development of Asian universities or countries. Put differently, if reputation rankings promote Global South universities' eagerness to reach the competitive levels of their Global North counterparts, what role does reputation ranking play in the economic development of poor countries in Asia, for instance?

As evidenced by government policies (Lee, Liu, & Wu, 2020), there seems to be a lack of understanding concerning reputation rankings and the meaning of 'world-class' universities in Asia. The question, therefore, remains: what is the meaning of 'world-class' universities to Asian countries? Does the rhetoric on 'world-class' universities mean development for Asia, promotion of international mobility (Oleksiyenko, Chan, Kim, Lo, & Manning, 2021), or assertion of colonial power in knowledge production (see Siltaoja, Juusola, & Kivijärvi, 2019; Altbach, 2013a)? What is known, however, is that the reputation rankings model promotes capitalism, where the powerful dictates winners and losers. Consequently, the monopoly of knowledge and its dissemination has been challenged in the United States (Hong & Rowell, 2019) and by academics from the global South. Just as any market, the ranking market continues to influence and reorder policy orientation to create a few powerful universities and winners in the North.

According to the 2020 QS World University Rankings report, the top 10 Asian universities were located in Singapore, Hong Kong (SAR), Mainland China, and South Korea (Lane, 2021). These countries are reported to have steady economic growth and have invested heavily in their higher education systems, especially in China (Altbach, 2013b). It should be noted that government policies have promoted and stimulated growth in national income and investment in higher education. Since policies depict higher education as an agent of development, reputation rankings become a promoting tool to attract more investors for further economic growth. Subsequently, countries in Southeast Asia are also prioritizing large investments in higher education (Rizvi, 2017) to improve rankings and development, since global rankings criteria favor high-resourced universities (Millot, 2015). While inequality in higher education can be attributed to ranking as one of its causal factors, ranking activities also showcase the vast resources available in Asian countries and the willingness of governments to finance their education system.

However, high investment in higher education for improved reputation rankings could be used to propagate political agendas and stimulate economic growth. With many Asian countries being industrial, government high investments in higher education could be interpreted as a political strategy or an attempt to gain more power. This pursuit of prosperity and economic upswing explains universities need to incorporate industry demands in their curricula and programs without consideration for individual aspiration graduates' creativity. Surely, this approach is not specific to Asia, but is a global issue caused by the reputation narrative and the drive to compete for status created by rankings.

2 Debriefing Rankings

Rankings' aims, methodology, and relevancy have been questioned by different authors (see Altbach, 2012; Fauzi, Tan, Daud, & Awalludin, 2020). Considering this discussion from a different perspective, the question of relevancy should be framed around ranking indicators in Asia. Among other criteria, the pursuit of excellence factors in both the QS and THE ranking indicators (Jeremic & Jovanovic-Milenkovic, 2014). Answering the question of relevancy is therefore essential to understand whether rankings indicators disrupt the structure and governance of higher education in the Asian region. While reputation rankings have become popular in Asia, higher education administrators in Asia pacific will need to reflect on the possible impact of ranking activities and culture of compliance on academics' workload (see Welch, 2016; Leung, 2007). Naturally, compliance with ranking criteria to achieve reputation can be time-consuming and costly for university management. A desire to remain relevant in Asian rankings could lead to extreme focus being placed on rankings indicators at the expense of students and staff needs. Furthermore, undue pressure could be exerted on academic staff to produce journal articles with international collaboration and for good citations (see Welch, 2016; Leung, 2007). Therefore, reputation rankings and indicators may contribute to our understanding of university governance, performance, and reform.

There is a general assumption that the Academic Ranking of World Universities (ARWU), QS World University Rankings (QSWUR), and Times Higher Education World University Rankings (THEWUR) ranking indicators reflect the quality and excellence in higher education governance (Soh, 2015b). This assumption generates some level of confusion regarding the measurement and assessment of quality in higher education, in general. In East Asia, the quality of higher education is often perceived by how quickly graduates can get jobs (Mok & Jiang, 2018). Another indicator is the performance of ranked universities' students in professional board examinations (see Matsuno, 2009). On the other hand, Asian graduates require to have their qualifications further assessed through programs such as Advanced Placement (AP) for further studies in North America for example (see Judson & Hobson, 2015). The purpose of the evaluation and assessment is to determine whether Asian universities' curriculum is on par with the quality of the host institutions. What's more, assessment agencies often use reputation rankings to determine degree equivalency (Hou, Hill, Chan, Chen, & Tang, 2021). Meanwhile, many of the Southeast Asian qualifications including professional licenses are not considered to be equivalent to any European and North American qualifications based on rankings (Sirat, Azman, & Bakar, 2016). For this reason, achieving ranking status is significant in Asian universities.

The weight carried by national and global rankings also informs Asian research-intensive institutions' choice of academics. Reputation rankings put pressure on academics to publish. However, most high-impact academic journals and editorial board members are academics from well-ranked universities or elite universities in Europe or North America (Goyanes & De-Marcos, 2020). This is attributable to the fact that journals use ranked institutions and academics from these institutions for reputation and to show the power of knowledge. As such, QS rankings and other ranking agencies place importance on research collaboration and peer-review (Hazelkorn, 2008). The university reputation rankings continue to favor editorial boards and western journals, which function as gatekeepers that determine essential knowledge as well as who gets the opportunity to publish (see Xie, Wu, & Li, 2019). Coincidentally, there is constant pressure from university administration on the need to produce journal articles capable of generating international recognition in terms of citations (Ambos, Mäkelä, Birkinshaw, & d'Este, 2008). Similarly, many of the not-well-resourced institutions tend to join the game of reputation rankings for recognition purposes. This race to publish and be recognized internationally places considerable strain on universities' academic staff as they seek to break into the cabal of journals that are predominantly western (Burgess & Shaw, 2010) with very few editorial board members from developing countries or unranked universities. Hedding and Breetzke (2021) note that academics and universities from the Global South constitute only 5%, as opposed to nearly 80% of editorial board members of the 5,202 journals in their study. This situation not only requires an examination of rankings indicators but also inequalities further deepened through the activities of reputation rankings to be revealed. On the other hand, ranking agencies such as QS are trying to improve the fairness of their criteria and the representativeness of their indicators (Sowter, Hijazi, & Reggio, 2017). Nevertheless, the improvement process requires transparency and inclusivity to ensure equality in global knowledge production and dissemination.

Perhaps the improvement of reputation rankings should start with making the controversial terminologies of world-class universities explicit. What all these terminologies suggest to universities in need of recognition is for them to align their operations to that of the so-called 'world-class' universities to benefit from being included in the league table of rankings. This includes making changes to the language of instruction, recruiting international professors, and requesting academic departments to promote international culture in their teachings to attract foreign students, among others. In other words, being a 'world-class' university signifies adopting Western operations, cultural identity, and governance. For instance, very few ranked, Asian universities are required to divert or redirect their resources to create a global identity within their national culture and institution because their learning environment and governance policies are constantly transforming historically ancient Asian institutions such as those in China into American and European universities (Li, 2012). However, ranking agencies did not consider 'world-class' universities to refer to universities in Asia or the Global South. Yet, the oldest university in the world, the University of Al Quaraquiyine, was founded in Fez, Morocco in 895 CE by Fatima bint Muhammad Al-Fihriya Al-Qurashiya (Stone, 2020). Evidently, this means that the Global South plays an important role in the foundation of knowledge and world civilization. Hence, ranking agencies should not regard universities in the Global South as being new to knowledge production.

There are many lessons to learn from Asian universities in relation to rankings, knowledge production, and dissemination. Evidence points to the fact that globalization and rankings may have been used as instruments to continue knowledge dominance and power by the West. If inclusivity and equity are taken into account in rankings, indicators and rankings criteria should consider the history and cultural identity of all universities in the Asian region and other developing countries in their assessment and review. It means history and identity during a QS review, for instance, should include the dynamics of faculty-student ratio, citations per faculty, and the proportion of international faculty to students. This will discourage universities in the Global South from viewing globalization as a goal to aspire to, but they will rather see it as a collegial exercise to promote quality, without losing their unique cultural identity. Thus, ARWU, QS, and THE ranking systems criteria and weighting may require synergy (see Chowdhury & Rahman, 2021) to ensure the reform of global higher education rankings.

3 Rephrasing Misconceptions in Rankings

There is a growing debate about the fact that rankings and their indicators misconstruct the realities of Asian countries, as evidenced by Japanese universities (Ishikawa, 2009). The misconception of indicators is partly intentional, and is, in a way, the capitalist agenda of higher education systems. Various reasons could explain why ranking brings about a sense of confusion in higher education globally (see Chen & Liao, 2012). Firstly, the controversies and misconceptions around rankings could be due to the fact that rankings outcomes determine good research for universities in Asia. Producing research with good citations favors Science and universities with the capacity to have large Science departments or faculties. Secondly, the confusion is that rankings show the unequal capacity of various universities to compete for reputation but with the same set of criteria. Likewise, the ability to attract international students and academics could mean a brain-drain to developing countries because rich universities from the West are getting the best of Asia, for instance. Alas, the two-way flow of knowledge from Global North to Global South is poorly analyzed. Disrupting Western universities' monopoly on the 'word class' status could occur by the non-participation of countries in the Global South in ranking activities. The withdrawal of developing countries from such activities would lead to ranking league tables becoming redundant and to developed countries seeming boastful. Therefore, the reexamination of certain assumptions may cause a change in the outlook for the top best 100 universities in the future.

Similarly, QS rankings have placed great emphasis on reputation and have been challenged for this fact (Huang, 2012). The term reputation distorts the objective of rankings in developing countries (Dill, 2009), since rankings indicators can be easily achieved for elite universities with a reputation for their long history of research, teaching, and funding. Evaluation and assessment of these elite universities with indicators that reflect their culture is almost like rubber-stamping the obvious. In other words, ranking criteria are designed based on the existing reputational factors of these universities. Elite universities can exert power over domestic admission policies to stay more relevant in national rankings as seen in the case of China (see Yan, 2020) where rural students struggled for admission slots. Said power comes in the form of Western universities' ability to influence policies on admission by ensuring that entrance into their programs is not only based on Asian minorities' academic prowess, but on the reputation of applicants or their families (see Espenshade, Chung, & Walling, 2004). This process ensures the continuity of the elite status of the institutions that ultimately favor reputation ranking criteria. By this, reputation protection has made elite universities in the Global North and South determine who will become their alumni. This may be the reason certain programs are almost designed to attract top politicians, actors, and people in a position of power to preserve the elitist status of the world-class universities. These categories of students can pay high tuition fees and maintain the financial reputation of these universities. Therefore, the peer-review method of world university rankings in terms of reputation will continue to favor universities that are evaluated by their colleagues. Unfortunately, these opportunities are unavailable to historically black institutions, community colleges, institutions, or students in poor communities and universities with alumni of lower status. Thus, reputation ranking seems discriminatory and perpetuates the exertion of power over powerless institutions and countries. In the global rankings, reputation rhetoric attracts the international student body to Western universities despite high tuition fees. Consequently, globalization and rankings become instruments in the colonialization of the Asian region.

For country-specific rankings, stability in politics, economics, and universities' ability to conduct research are primordial (Pietrucha, 2018). While rankings represent another instrument of control in international university relations, corruption has also allowed its influence to be deepened among Asian universities. Perhaps corruption in higher education governance threatens quality in both East and Southeast Asian countries (Welch, A2020). Ergo, higher education in Southeast Asia requires effective leadership and policies at the national level to be globally competitive and locally relevant (see Marginson, 2006). While development takes time, global rankings may continue to take advantage of weak government policies in Asia to dictate and direct the mission of higher education systems using rankings criteria. Poor infrastructure and poor funding need to improve for the majority of Asian universities to attain the status of the so-called 'world-class universities' (Marginson, 2012).

The continued argument against rankings is that they are statistically biased towards institutions of different characteristics (Moed, 2017). This argument can assist us in understanding not only the statistical design and analysis of rankings problematics but also in knowing the decision-makers behind the attribution of the 'world-class' university status, who are often not from developing countries (see Lo, 2011). The criteria, indicators, weighing, and general methodology of rankings are likely to represent the views of the elite from so-called 'world-class' universities. This process creates bias and an unfair process for the non-participating groups in society because of the lack of representation in policy formulation for the criteria used to evaluate their universities and their research.

Therefore, rankings should be able to influence stakeholders and industry towards innovation (Pavel, 2015). Innovations are possible with the participation of all stakeholders in society. Innovation starts at the national level and should reflect citizens' well-being. On the other hand, rankings seem to determine policy outlooks and on the focus of a country in terms of innovation. Still, the race to be reputable may have left citizens behind in the development process of their countries as national universities offer internationally appealing programs with no relevance to national development. One can, thus, safely conclude that citizens may be focusing on studying programs that cannot promote their intellectual ability or be useful in society. Politics and government policies seem to expect universities to focus on programs that align with certain political agenda in exchange for funding. The complication at the national level and misalignment of universities' mission to society continue to provide opportunities for rankings to control universities in developing countries. For instance, if Southeast Asia and ASEAN universities could commit a significant percentage of the national budget to develop national universities with the aim to create a unique identity, these institutions could likely provide solutions to climate change, food shortage, inequality, poverty, all without reputation rankings criteria. For other developing countries, university rankings are insignificant if poverty and system inequality remain pervasive.

Hence, performance measurement, rankings, and accreditation of universities globally are deeply problematic for higher education governance. These agencies have created situations where the purpose of higher education is now to tick boxes and to count knowledge in terms of research dissemination. Rewards are bestowed upon academics not for the quality of their research but based on the number of journal publications. Moreover, rewards for citations happen to be given mostly to academics from elite world-class universities with strong international collaboration. In North America, adjunct professors' appointments are common. Though universities are not obliged to keep professors or offer them a substantial remuneration package to retain them, their profile remains useful for universities' reputation rankings. Since attracting high profile professors is costly in Asia (Yudkevich, Altbach, & Rumbley, 2017), universities are often compelled to direct their institutional resources to gain ranking with such appointments. Academics' performance indicators operate similarly to rankings criteria in that promotion and performance bonuses are also based on whether academics achieved ranking and accreditation agencies' criteria. Universities with reputation rankings attract strong academics but often, these institutions face employee retention issues due to a heavy workload and salary dissatisfaction. High staff turnover is common in developing countries once universities gain the so-called reputation ranking in the global ranking league table Because university administrators seem to pay less attention to staff as well as their [the staff] contributions to the achieved ranking status. It could be argued that rankings may have instilled deception within higher education and is conducive to a capitalist agenda in universities of high status.

4 Analysis of QS Reputation Rankings in Asia

To put the discussion on reputation rankings into a concrete perspective, data from the Quacquarrelli Symonds (QS) World University Rankings reports were analyzed. The analysis includes 587 selected institutions from Asian higher education institutions that have participated in 2012, 2013, 2018, 2019 and 2020 and been evaluated in the process of determining "world-class" reputation status (see Table 1 and the Appendix).

4.1 Data Collection based on QS World University Rankings Reports

The descriptive statistics and performance analysis based on universities' status, size, age, focus, and research were analyzed to advance the arguments in the literature on factors influencing rankings academic reputation, employer reputation, faculty score, citation per faculty, and international students score. The following equation shows the model used for the analysis:

$$\text{Overall Score}_{it} = \alpha_0 + \alpha_1 \text{ Size} + \alpha_2 \text{ Focus} + \alpha_3 \text{ Research} + \alpha_4 \text{ Age} + \alpha_5 \text{ Status} + \varepsilon_i$$

$$\text{Overall Score}_{it} = \alpha_0 + \alpha_1 \text{ Academic Reputation Rank} + \alpha_2 \text{ Employer Reputation Rank} + \alpha_3 \text{ Faculty Student Rank} + \alpha_4 \text{ Citations per Faculty Rank} + \alpha_5 \text{ International Faculty Rank} + \alpha_6 \text{ International Students Rank} + \varepsilon_i$$

The analysis assumed that unobserved institutions influence the overall score. Therefore, the analysis takes into account the effect of unobserved institution-specific characteristics using fixed effect and random effect techniques. While

TABLE 1 QS World University Rankings data

Year	Number of institutions	Percentage	Cumulative
2012[a]	111	18.91	18.91
2013[b]	101	17.21	36.12
2018[c]	120	20.44	56.56
2019[c]	126	21.46	78.02
2020[c]	129	21.98	100
Total	587	100	

a https://www.yumpu.com/en/document/read/28752334/qs-world-university-rankingsr
b https://www.qs.com/wp-content/uploads/2013/09/2013QSWUR_supplement-Copy.pdf
c https://www.kaggle.com/datasets/divyansh22/qs-world-university-rankings

some variables, age for instance, are continuous, others, such as size, focus, research, and status, are categorical in nature. The sizes considered are extra-large (XL), large (L), medium (M), and small (S), which are recoded as 3, 2, 1, and 0, respectively. Focus consists of FC (Fully comprehensive), CO (Comprehensive), FO (Focused), and SP (Special), which are coded as 3, 2, 1, and 0, respectively. Research is represented as VH (Very High), HI (High), and MD (Medium), which equate to 2, 1, and 0, respectively. Status represents 'A' as public institutions, 'B' as private institutions and recoded as A = 1 and B = 2. For the purpose of this chapter, the analysis emphasizes the ability of Asian institutions in meeting the criteria of research and internationalization in QS ranking indicators. The subsequent chapters provide a comprehensive analysis of QS metrics, methodology, and indicators used in ranking higher education institutions in Asia.

4.2 Regression for Institutions' Size, Focus, Research, Age Status and Log of Citations per Faculty Rank

Table 2 presents the estimation of *size, focus, research, age, and status* of the citations per faculty rank using ordinary least squares (OLS). While the *focus*

TABLE 2 Regression for institutional characteristics and citations per faculty rank

Variables	OLS citations per faculty rank[a]
Size	0.150*
	(0.0886)
Focus	0.313***
	(0.0899)
Research	−0.812**
	(0.409)
Age	−0.131*
	(0.0726)
Status	−0.612***
	(0.183)
Constant	7.364***
	(0.879)
Observations	310
R-squared	0.124

***$p < 0.01$, **$p < 0.05$, *$p < 0.1$
a Standard errors in parentheses.

has a significant positive relationship with the citations per faculty rank, the *size* has a positive relationship with the citations per faculty rank, but it is not statistically significant. Whereas *research* has a significant negative association with citations per faculty rank, the *status* has a negative and significant association with citations per faculty rank. Similarly, *age* has a negative and significant association with citations per faculty rank. In this case, the *focus* and *size* of institutions determines the ability to achieve reputation rankings in Asia. The results illustrated in table indicate that the *focus* and *size* of 568 institutions influences citation per academic score. Institutions status such as public or private is insignificant in citations per faculty score. It can, therefore, be deduced from these results that reputation status is historically determined, and resources are linked to institutions' ability to support the research of their academic staff. The likelihood of academics from big institutions having access to international projects and co-authorship opportunities is possible because of their reputation. In this case, an institution's status in terms of public or private cannot affect the quality of research and productivity of academic staff. Thereby, the reputation of big institutions with good academic focus may continue to assist their reputation ranking status on the QS table. The significance of these results for small institutions or largely teaching institutions in Asia is that they convey Asian institutions' need to either collaborate with academics from big institutions for recognition or bow out of the ranking race. Essentially, institutions of different *sizes* and academic *focus* cannot compete equally in terms of reputation rankings.

While *sizes* and *focus* remain significant for faculty in terms of research dissemination and reputation, the results show that research published by the top 100 institutions in Asia are likely to be cited more on average than institutions outside these categories. However, it is interesting to note that the top institutions' research was not well cited per faculty score. Though most of these institutions have produced significant research due to their sizes, they have fallen short in terms of citations.

4.3 *Regression of Size, Focus, Research, Age, Status and Log of International Faculty Rank*

Table 3 presents the estimation of *size, focus, research, age, and status* on the international faculty rank using ordinary least squares (OLS). Variables such as *focus* and *status* have a negative and significant association with international faculty rank. While the *size, research, and age* have a positive and significant association with the international faculty rank. It means the *size, research* and *age* of the institutions constitute the ability to attract international faculty or researchers that may have assisted them in increasing their research output

TABLE 3 Institutional characteristics and international faculty rank

Variables	OLS international faculty rank[a]
Size	0.243**
	(0.103)
Focus	−0.330***
	(0.108)
Research	0.282**
	(0.111)
Age	0.588***
	(0.0784)
Status	−0.380**
	(0.179)
Constant	3.417***
	(0.456)
Observations	320
R-squared	0.246

***$p < 0.01$, **$p < 0.05$, *$p < 0.1$
a Standard errors in parentheses.

and citations. Therefore, the largest and oldest institutions with research capacity are well-positioned to meet the criteria of internationalization in QS ranking indicators. The results further indicate that the top 100 institutions have more international faculty, which could be a causal factor in their ability to collaborate and produce more research. Still, research citations do not only indicate feasibility but also the relevance of the research produced among the international community. This means that the *age*, *size* and *research* of top 100 institutions can attract international faculty but does not guarantee citations if their research does not align with their peers' research interests. Indeed, high citation numbers depend on the focus of these institutions and the choice of journals for publications.

The top 100 institutions are older in terms of history. Results demonstrate that older institutions have a higher chance of getting good rankings. The age of the institutions also correlates with effective structure, management, and operation of academic programs which may ultimately result in high reputation rankings in terms of indicators.

4.4 *Regression of Rank Indicators on the Log of the Overall Score*

Column 1 in Table 4 is the estimation of academic reputation rank, employer reputation rank, faculty-student rank, citations per faculty rank international faculty rank and international students rank on the overall score using ordinary least squares (OLS). The variables such as academic reputation rank, employer reputation rank, faculty-student rank, citations per faculty rank, and international faculty rank have a negative and significant association with the overall score. Notwithstanding, the international student rank has a negative relationship with the overall score, but is insignificant. Meanwhile, column 2 presents the estimation of academic reputation rank, employer reputation

TABLE 4   Regression of rank indicators on the log of the overall score

Variables	OLS log of overall score[a]	Fixed effect log of overall score[a]	Random effect log of overall score[a]
Log of academic reputation rank	−0.146***	−0.215***	−0.198***
	(0.0260)	(0.0239)	(0.0197)
Log of employer reputation rank	−0.0541**	−0.0442*	−0.0503***
	(0.0236)	(0.0240)	(0.0194)
Log of faculty student rank	−0.0957***	−0.0556***	−0.0675***
	(0.0176)	(0.0179)	(0.0141)
Log of citations per faculty rank	−0.0786***	−0.0428***	−0.0475***
	(0.0137)	(0.00906)	(0.00809)
Log of international faculty rank	−0.0279*	−0.0653*	−0.0511***
	(0.0147)	(0.0356)	(0.0149)
Log of international students rank	−0.0345	0.00585	−0.000158
	(0.0231)	(0.0183)	(0.0145)
Constant	6.234***	6.076***	6.067***
	(0.127)	(0.207)	(0.109)
Observations	105	105	105
R-squared	0.894	0.808	
Number of code		48	48
sigma_u		0.108	0.100
sigma_e		0.0311	0.0311
rho		0.923	0.912

***$p < 0.01$, **$p < 0.05$, *$p < 0.1$
a   Standard errors in parentheses.

rank, faculty-student rank, citations per faculty rank, international faculty rank, and international students rank on the overall score using a fixed-effect model or technique. The academic reputation rank, employer reputation rank, faculty-student rank and citations per faculty rank, and international faculty rank have a negative and significant effect on the overall score. While International student rank has a positive and insignificant influence on the overall score or ranking. Column 3 presents the estimation of academic reputation rank, employer reputation rank, faculty-student rank, citations per faculty rank international faculty rank and international students rank on the overall score using a random-effect model or technique. The academic reputation rank, employer reputation rank, faculty Student rank and citations per faculty rank, and international faculty rank have a negative and significant effect on the overall score. While international student rank has a negative and insignificant influence on the overall score or ranking. Finally, the Hausman test is an asymptotic chi-square test ($p > \chi^2 = 0.256$), which presents whether fixed-effect or random effect is accepted. The Hausman test shows that χ^2 is not statistically significant, thus, the random effect is preferred for the study of Asian higher institution rankings.

Table 4 indicates that academic reputation improves the overall score of highly ranked institutions, which can be attributed to their internationalization activities. These results are congruent with the analysis in the literature and the reason why indicators of ranking seem to favor elite universities with a strong international profile. Most elite and 'world-class' status belong to the top 100 universities. However, their reputation score may not be attributable to QS indicators of rankings only. Table 4 also showcases interesting results concerning institutions' reputation part in attracting international students. Interestingly, private institutions could attract international students compared to public, where one would expect the opposite to occur i.e., public-status institutions to attract more international students. However, another contributing factor for public institutions could be the decline in public funding for higher education as well as the changes in international student mobility caused by the reputation rankings could have changed students' mobility from high-status universities to medium and low-status institutions. It is essential that policies which make allowances for the current global financial crisis affecting Asian countries be implemented to create a sense of trust beyond status for international students.

4.5 *Politics of Scholarship in Rankings*
The results of the analysis show that knowledge is still controlled by a few elite universities (see Bracco Bruce, 2022) although the dynamic is changing due to

spending and investment in knowledge creation in Asia. What is considered knowledge by former colonies and their universities is what the West defines it to be (see Grosfoguel, 2013) as can be seen in ranking criteria which show how the status and age of institutions influence reputation rankings in Asia. The globalization of knowledge is the idea of the West, which have been further consolidated by knowledge 'residing' in the Global North for several years. The status quo has been greatly challenged by scholars (Lo, 2011) from the South, who urge academics in developing countries to create knowledge and scholarship that will reflect their legacies and realities independent from Western European and North American epistemologies. Researchers such as Mignolo (2009) called this phenomenon "white knowledge". Globalization movements and global university rankings have made this type of writing difficult in Asia as rankings criteria benchmark for higher education performance. This type of restrictions on publication types show that southern epistemological access is still constrained and controlled by ideas of internationalization, globalization, and ranking systems. While the globalization of knowledge is needed, its relevance for Asian institutions in terms of identity, language and culture is not very clear in the analysis.

Fundamentally, the question of knowledge and who determines it is crucial to modern civilization. The technology and knowledge transfer are, for instance, determined by many technical institutes or universities in North America and Western Europe. Collaboration is still difficult for universities in Asia as low-status institutions are unable to produce more research. Interestingly, they are able to get more citations and international students as depicted in the results above. This shows that ranking criteria may not necessarily influence research excellence, and that there could be other institutional factors influencing reputation. However, high-status institutions may be hesitant to collaborate with universities of low status that do not figure on the ranking table. Nevertheless, the analysis indicates that this is immaterial as other factors could help low-status institutions to perform better in research. The argument is that if the transfer of knowledge and global development characterize globalization then, better collaboration between high-status universities and low-status universities could only be beneficial. However, the apparent trend remains collaboration between universities of similar status. Indeed, it is unlikely to see western universities determining the goals of academic projects, research, and knowledge dissemination of funded work for academics and universities from developing countries. Universities from Asian countries require improved status as well as funding to conduct quality research. Since knowledge creation and dissemination are largely determined by the funders, western journals, and policies of the universities on the ranking league table, the best researchers of the

Global South migrate to the Global North through international academic fellowships or student mobility programs. The implications of such movements for Southern epistemologies are that the globalization of rankings will remain a crucial factor for the West to maintain its hegemony on knowledge.

Accordingly, Southern epistemologies should challenge the features of managerialism and neo-liberal policies in the governance of their higher education systems. Otherwise stated, Southern epistemologies need regional collaboration with no or little interference of ranking criteria. The researchers from the Global South may be more inclined towards journals outside their country of origin, due to ranking, reputation, and status, among other reasons. This occurrence has been termed academic imperialism and/or injustice in knowledge production by most colonial researchers.

For instance, most members on the editorial board and publications of top academic journals hail from the Global north (Collins & Verdier, 2018) compared to Asian-based researchers (Horta, 2018). With such a low Global South publication percentage, one can understand why researchers and universities in other developing countries do not feature well in international publications. Factors such as inadequate funding may have affected researchers and research production in the Global south (Espin, Palmas, Carrasco-Rueda, Riemer, Allen, Berkebile, & Bruna, 2017). The few academics who managed to publish may have experienced different forms of discrimination and injustice (Bou Zeineddine, Saab, Lášticová, Kende, & Ayanian, 2022) based on their language, nationality, focus, or title of the article, which are all based on the impression that Southern epistemologies and publications may be inferior.

For several decades and until the recent century, the debate on who holds the monopoly on knowledge has been very complex and has triggered several articles. This complexity is recognized in the knowledge production of colonialism and postcolonialism discourse. For instance, postcolonial researchers look for a renewal of the mind through knowledge that reflects the uniqueness of national identity, culture, and national development. This also includes rethinking colonial curricula, language used in producing knowledge, and knowledge usage for development purposes.

The history of knowledge and colonialism, however, cannot be erased but can inform the creation and promotion of independence in the global transfer of knowledge. Yet, greater challenges still remain in the forms of the deception of globalization and ranking systems. Rankings trigger a sense and feeling of inadequacy in academics of the Global South, which leads to higher value and consideration being placed on Western academics as the only models of excellence and good reputation. It is, therefore, important to reflect on the process of knowledge production before and after colonialization, particularly since literature shows that little progress has been made thus far in this regard. The future of higher education is dire indeed should knowledge and its dissemination be only monopolized by the West through instruments such as globalization and rankings.

The marketization and commercialization of knowledge have also become popular due to global rankings, which engenders competition for recognition. The extent of this issue in Asia is portrayed by the excessive resource allocation for publications at the expense of knowledge transformation. In addition, the knowledge creation market happens to be largely controlled by countries that also determine what is considered knowledge. What is more, funding to conduct research and publish is key to knowledge production and academic success. However, the bulk of funding opportunities can be found in North America or Europe. Hence, the need to gain access to limited funding undeniably dilutes research focus before the research process even begins.

Thereupon, pressure to publish and to receive funding for research continue to create unethical practices and compromises the quality of the knowledge produced by scholars over the years. One critical point is that: the management and governance of higher education are overseen by managers, knowledge is viewed as a quantifiable entity, and reward is given on the grounds of the number of publications and not necessarily the quality. Unfortunately, this situation led to the proliferation of predatory journals globally. This argument is critical of the market approach to knowledge production in research publications. Once more, it is essential that rankings, rankers, and ranked seek possible ways to facilitate North-South collaboration in knowledge sharing, acknowledging the fact that ranking has become an urge business and that the market is controlled by powerful academics and universities.

Global competitiveness in higher education is facilitated by collaboration, which can include academics and student exchanges. This type of academic activity has strengthened ties between institutions and enhanced the reputation status of many institutions in the developing world. The most common hindrance to higher education institutions being globally competitive is that ranked universities and academics from leading universities are only amenable to collaboration with similar institutions. This promotes the creation of a cabal in higher education and the continuation of dominance of ranked and high-status universities in the rankings system. Universities with low or no rankings may need to negotiate harder, as well as alter their university core mandate to have access to collaboration opportunities in the hopes of eventually meeting the requirements of the Western universities or ranked universities. Such collaborations often require a few strong academics and students in developing countries to avail themselves. An example of such an endeavor is an academic exchange program that requires the international faculty to pay bench fees and/or pay for all fees for the duration of their collaborative research, thus allowing them access to the resources of the universities in the West.

Another critical point is to determine the reason behind the limited or lack of collaboration between low-ranked universities. This phenomenon could be attributed to an over-reliance on access to Western epistemology and to the race among the top-ranked universities in the world. Though western ranking organizations have not stratified collaboration among local universities of low ranking, they have propagated the wrong narrative of western endorsement of international collaboration being the major criteria to score high on the status category in the ranking assessment.

One crucial question posed in this chapter is why developing countries find it challenging to redress the major issues of inequality and inequity in reputation rankings. The literature in this field is crowded with different thoughts on the contexts influencing epistemic justice or injustice perception and the problematic nature of World University Rankings in an Asian higher education setting.

References

Ambos, T. C., Mäkelä, K., Birkinshaw, J., & d'Este, P. (2008). When does university research get commercialized? Creating ambidexterity in research institutions. *Journal of management Studies*, 45(8), 1424–1447.

Altbach, P. G. (2012). The globalization of college and university rankings. *Change: The Magazine of Higher Learning*, 44(1), 26–31.

Altbach, P. G. (2013a). Advancing the national and global knowledge economy: the role of research universities in developing countries. *Studies in Higher Education*, 38(3), 316–330.

Altbach, P. G. (2013b). Hong Kong's academic advantage. In P. G. Altbach (Ed.), *The international imperative in higher education* (pp. 89–93). Sense.

Altbach, P. G., Reisberg, L., & Rumbley, L. E. (2019). *Trends in global higher education: Tracking an academic revolution*. Brill.

Bracco Bruce, L. (2022). Coloniality of power and coloniality of knowledge: Prisons in Peru as post-colonial and patriarchal institutions. In L. Bracco Bruce (Ed.), *Prison in Peru* (pp. 33–71). Palgrave Macmillan.

Bou Zeineddine, F., Saab, R., Lášticová, B., Kende, A., & Ayanian, A. H. (2022). "Some uninteresting data from a faraway country": Inequity and coloniality in international social psychological publications. *Journal of Social Issues*, 78(2), 320–345.

Chen, K. H., & Liao, P. Y. (2012). A comparative study on world university rankings: A bibliometric survey. *Scientometrics*, 92(1), 89–103.

Chowdhury, A. R., & Rahman, Z. (2021). Global ranking framework & indicators of higher educational institutions: A comparative study. *Library Philosophy and Practice*, 1–8.

Collier, S. (2021). *World university rankings – frequently asked questions*. Retrieved April 24, 2022, from https://www.topuniversities.com/university-rankings-articles/world-university-rankings/world-university-rankings-frequently-asked-questions

Collins, S. L., & Verdier, J. M. (2018). Editorial boards must be internationally representative. *BioScience, 68*(4), 235–235.

Dill, D. D. (2009). Convergence and diversity: The role and influence of university rankings. In D. Dill (Ed.), *University rankings, diversity, and the new landscape of higher education* (pp. 97–116). Brill.

Espenshade, T. J., Chung, C. Y., & Walling, J. L. (2004). Admission preferences for minority students, athletes, and legacies at elite universities. *Social Science Quarterly, 85*(5), 1422–1446.

Espin, J., Palmas, S., Carrasco-Rueda, F., Riemer, K., Allen, P. E., Berkebile, N., & Bruna, E. M. (2017). A persistent lack of international representation on editorial boards in environmental biology. *PLoS biology, 15*(12), e2002760.

Fauzi, M. A., Tan, C. N. L., Daud, M., & Awalludin, M. M. N. (2020). University rankings: A review of methodological flaws. *Issues in Educational Research*.

Goyanes, M., & De-Marcos, L. (2020). Academic influence and invisible colleges through editorial board interlocking in communication sciences: A social network analysis of leading journals. *Scientometrics, 123*(2), 791–811.

Grosfoguel, R. (2013). The structure of knowledge in westernised universities: Epistemic racism/sexism and the four genocides/epistemicides. *Human Architecture: Journal of the sociology of self-knowledge, 1*(1), 73–90.

Hawkins, J. N. (2010). Higher education transformation: Some trends in California and Asia. In J. Jacob & D. Neubauer (Eds.), *The search for new governance of higher education in Asia* (pp. 29–47). Palgrave Macmillan.

Hazelkorn, E. (2008). Learning to live with league tables and ranking: The experience of institutional leaders. *Higher Education Policy, 21*(2), 193–215.

Hazelkorn, E. (2015). *Rankings and the reshaping of higher education: The battle for world-class excellence*. Springer.

Hedding, D. W., & Breetzke, G. (2021). "Here be dragons!" The gross under-representation of the Global South on editorial boards in Geography. *The Geographical Journal, 187*(4), 331–345.

Hong, E., & Rowell, L. (2019). Challenging knowledge monopoly in education in the US through democratizing knowledge production and dissemination. *Educational Action Research, 27*(1), 125–143.

Hou, A. Y. C., Hill, C., Chan, S. J., Chen, D. I. R., & Tang, M. (2021). Is quality assurance relevant to overseas qualification recognition in Asian higher education? Examining the regulatory framework and the roles of quality assurance agencies and professional accreditors. *Journal of Education and Work, 34*(3), 373–387.

Hou, A. Y. C., Hill, C., Hu, Z., & Lin, L. (2022). What is driving Taiwan government for policy change in higher education after the year of 2016 – in search of egalitarianism or pursuit of academic excellence? *Studies in Higher Education, 47*(2), 338–351.

Horta, H. (2018). Higher-education researchers in Asia: The risks of insufficient contribution to international higher-education research. In *Researching higher education in Asia* (pp. 15–36). Springer.

Huang, M. H. (2011). A comparison of three major academic rankings for world universities: From a research evaluation perspective. *Journal of Library & Information Studies, 9*(1).

Huang, M. H. (2012). Opening the black box of QS world university rankings. *Research Evaluation, 21*(1), 71–78.

Ishikawa, M. (2009). University rankings, global models, and emerging hegemony: Critical analysis from Japan. *Journal of Studies in International Education, 13*(2), 159–173.

Jabjaimoh, P., Samart, K., Jansakul, N., & Jibenja, N. (2019). Optimization for better world university rank. *Journal of Scientometric Research, 8*(1), 18–20.

Jeremic, V., & Jovanovic-Milenkovic, M. (2014). Evaluation of Asian university rankings: Position and perspective of leading Indian higher education institutions. *Current Science*, 1647–1653.

Judson, E., & Hobson, A. (2015). Growth and achievement trends of Advanced Placement (AP) exams in American high schools. *American Secondary Education*, 59–76.

Lane, C. (2021). *Top 10 universities in Asia 2020*. Retrieved April 24, 2022, https://www.topuniversities.com/university-rankings-articles/asian-university-rankings/top-10-universities-asia-2020

Lee, J., Liu, K., & Wu, Y. (2020). Does the Asian catch-up model of world-class universities work? Revisiting the zero-sum game of global university rankings and government policies. *Educational Research for Policy and Practice, 19*(3), 319–343.

Leung, K. (2007). The glory and tyranny of citation impact: An East Asian perspective. *Academy of Management Journal, 50*(3), 510–513.

Li, J. (2012). World-class higher education and the emerging Chinese model of the university. *Prospects, 42*(3), 319–339.

Lo, W. Y. W. (2011). Soft power, university rankings and knowledge production: Distinctions between hegemony and self-determination in higher education. *Comparative Education, 47*(2), 209–222.

Marginson, S. (2006). Dynamics of national and global competition in higher education. *Higher Education, 52*(1), 1–39.

Marginson, S. (2012). Different roads to a shared goal: Political and cultural variation in world-class universities. In Q. I. Wang, C. Ying, & C. L. Nian (Eds.), *Building world-class universities* (pp. 11–33). Sense.

Marginson, S., & Van der Wende, M. (2007). To rank or to be ranked: The impact of global rankings in higher education. *Journal of studies in International Education, 11*(3–4), 306–329.

Maričić, M., Bulajić, M., Radojičić, Z., & Jeremić, V. (2016). Multivariate approach to imposing additional constraints on the benefit-of-the-doubt model: The case of QS world university rankings by subject. *Croatian Review of Economic, Business and Social Statistics, 2*(1), 1–14.

Matsuno, A. (2009). *Nurse migration: the Asian perspective*. ILO/EU Asian Programme on the Governance of Labour Migration.

Mignolo, W. D. (2009). Epistemic disobedience, independent thought and decolonial freedom. *Theory, Culture & Society, 26*(7–8), 159–181.

Millot, B. (2015). International rankings: Universities vs. higher education systems. *International Journal of Educational Development, 40*, 156–165.

Moed, H. F. (2017). A critical comparative analysis of five world university rankings. *Scientometrics, 110*(2), 967–990.

Mok, K. H., & Jiang, J. (2018). Massification of higher education and challenges for graduate employment and social mobility: East Asian experiences and sociological reflections. *International Journal of Educational Development, 63*, 44–51.

Ng, S. W. (2012). Rethinking the mission of internationalization of higher education in the Asia-Pacific region. *Compare: A Journal of Comparative and International Education, 42*(3), 439–459.

Oleksiyenko, A. V., Chan, S. J., Kim, S. K., Lo, W. Y. W., & Manning, K. D. (2021). World class universities and international student mobility: Repositioning strategies in the Asian Tigers. *Research in Comparative and International Education, 16*(3), 295–317.

Ortega, D., & Busch-Armendariz, N. (2014). Elite knowledge or the reproduction of the knowledge of privilege: Social work doctoral education. *Affilia, 29*(1), 5–7.

Pavel, A. P. (2015). Global university rankings-a comparative analysis. *Procedia Economics and Finance, 26*, 54–63.

Perkins, R., & Neumayer, E. (2014). Geographies of educational mobilities: Exploring the uneven flows of international students. *The Geographical Journal, 180*(3), 246–259.

Pietrucha, J. (2018). Country-specific determinants of world university rankings. *Scientometrics, 114*(3), 1129–1139.

Rizvi, F. (2017). Higher education in Southeast Asia. *Changing constellations of Southeast Asia: From Northeast Asia to China*, 65–83.

Shin, J. C., & Harman, G. (2009). New challenges for higher education: Global and Asia-Pacific perspectives. *Asia Pacific Education Review, 10*(1), 1–13.

Shin, J. C., & Toutkoushian, R. K. (2011). The past, present, and future of university rankings. In T. Aarrevaara & M. Finkelstein (Eds.), *University rankings* (pp. 1–16). Springer.

Siltaoja, M., Juusola, K., & Kivijärvi, M. (2019). 'World-class' fantasies: A neocolonial analysis of international branch campuses. *Organization, 26*(1), 75–97.

Sirat, M., Azman, N., & Bakar, A. A. (2016). Harmonization of higher education in Southeast Asia Regionalism: Politics first, and then education. In S. L. Robertson, K. Olds, R. Dale, & Q. A. Dang (Eds.), *Global regionalisms and higher education*. Edward Elgar Publishing.

Soh, K. C. (2015a). Multicolinearity and indicator redundancy problem in world university rankings: An example using times higher education world university ranking 2013–2014 data. *Higher Education Quarterly, 69*(2), 158–174. http://dx.doi.org/10.1111/hequ.12058

Soh, K. (2015b). What the Overall doesn't tell about world university rankings: Examples from ARWU, QSWUR, and THEWUR in 2013. *Journal of Higher Education Policy and Management, 37*(3), 295–307.

Sowter, B., Hijazi, S., & Reggio, D. (2017). Ranking world universities: A decade of refinement, and the road ahead. In K. Downing & J. F. A. Ganotice (Eds.), *World university rankings and the future of higher education* (pp. 1–24). IGI Global.

Stone, W (2020). *The world's first university was founded by a woman*. Global Academy Job.com. Retrieved April 24, 2022, from https://blog.globalacademyjobs.com/the-worlds-first-university-was-founded-by-a-woman/

Taylor, P., & Braddock, R. (2007). International university ranking systems and the idea of university excellence. *Journal of Higher Education Policy and Management, 29*(3), 245–260.

Tilak, J. B. (2015). Higher education in South Asia: Crisis and challenges. *Social Scientist, 43*(1/2), 43–59.

Vernon, M. M., Balas, E. A., & Momani, S. (2018). Are university rankings useful to improve research? A systematic review. *PloS One, 13*(3), e0193762.

Waltman, L., Wouters, P., & van Eck, N. J. (2017). *Ten principles for the responsible use of university rankings*. Retrieved September 24, 2019, from https://www.universiteitleiden.nl/binaries/content/assets/algemeen/onderzoek/responsible use of university-rankings.pdf

Welch, A. (2016). Audit culture and academic production. *Higher Education Policy, 29*(4), 511–538.

Welch, A. (2020). Of worms and woodpeckers: governance & corruption in East and Southeast Asian higher education. *Studies in Higher Education, 45*(10), 2073–2081.

Yan, K., & Wu, L. (2020). The adjustment concerns of rural students enrolled through special admission policy in elite universities in China. *Higher Education, 80*(2), 215–235.

CHAPTER 2

QS World University Rankings' Metrics Analysis

Abstract

Asia and its higher education policies need to recognize the implications of the metrics used for evaluating their institutions. This chapter analyzes QS data reports from five different years and argue how ranking results may contribute to systemic injustice regarding the power and politics of knowledge production in Asia. Ranking metrics and other categories were analyzed and discussed based on the availability of resources in developing Asian countries.

Keywords

QS World University Rankings – metrics – evaluations – analysis – higher education institutions – Asia

1 Introduction

Whether the performance of universities should be measured is a quality question. On the one hand, how, by whom, and what instruments should be used to measure universities of different characteristics requires a political debate (Berbegal-Mirabent & Ribeiro-Soriano, 2015; Schulze-Cleven, Reitz, Maesse, & Angermuller, 2017). On the other hand, universities should be able to demonstrate how they ensure quality in meeting society's demands. In this case, it is necessary to provide evidence of quality in the form of ratings and rankings to show the level of competitiveness of their academic programs. One of the most popular organizations that rate the performance of universities is the QS World University Rankings (Sowter, Reggio, & Hijazi, 2017). It uses distinct metrics and peer-review methods to judge the performance of participating universities globally (Huang, 2012). QS metrics and methodology have been challenged from different perspectives, yet, it remains one of the only ways to encourage universities to make quality one of their priorities. Though QS methodology may have created competition and put a strain on the management of higher education resources (Lee, Liu, & Wu, 2020), comparing universities from different regions remains relevant. It can be argued that ranking global universities can be complex and almost impossible to achieve without errors and bias. However, QS rankings seem to have demonstrated transparency through its six metrics and by a willingness to improve its assessment framework (Anowar, Helal, Afroj, Sultana, Sarker, & Mamun, 2015).

The changes that have occurred in the QS assessment framework, methodology and reporting may be the result of several publications that have challenged the ranking's process and method. The QS methodology considers institutions' size, focus, status, research, and the weighing category or metric in assessment processes. These factors are crucial as they may influence ranking results. The following tables and figures are from analyzing QS data collected from different years using Ordinary Least Squares (OLS) regression and other statistical methods. These methods were utilized to generate descriptive, correlation and regression statistics of variables patterns forming part of or potentially influencing metrics used by QS to rank Asian universities.

2   Modelling and Analysis of QS Ranking Methodologies

The analyses cover universities in Asia that are on the ranking table of QS for 2012, 2013, 2018, 2019 and 2020. These universities are evaluated based on QS reputation indicators and how each institution performed against the indicators based on the score of universities from the top 100 universities in Asia. The descriptive statistics, which include means and percentages of how universities performed, are considered to conclude the influence of university classification on their performance. To determine how rankings methods apply in practice, the QS reputation rankings are modelled and based on the equation below:

Faculty Student Score$_{it}$
$= \alpha_0 + \alpha_1 \text{ Size} + \alpha_2 \text{ Focus} + \alpha_3 \text{ Research} + \alpha_4 \text{ Age} + \alpha_5 \text{ Status} + \varepsilon_i$

Citations per Faculty Rank$_{it}$
$= \alpha_0 + \alpha_1 \text{ Size} + \alpha_2 \text{ Focus} + \alpha_3 \text{ Research} + \alpha_4 \text{ Age} + \alpha_5 \text{ Status} + \varepsilon_i$

International Faculty Score$_{it}$
$= \alpha_0 + \alpha_1 \text{ Size} + \alpha_2 \text{ Focus} + \alpha_3 \text{ Research} + \alpha_4 \text{ Age} + \alpha_5 \text{ Status} + \varepsilon_i$

International Student Score$_{it}$
$= \alpha_0 + \alpha_1 \text{ Size} + \alpha_2 \text{ Focus} + \alpha_3 \text{ Research} + \alpha_4 \text{ Age} + \alpha_5 \text{ Status} + \varepsilon_i$

International Student Rank$_{it}$
$$= \alpha_0 + \alpha_1 \text{ Size} + \alpha_2 \text{ Focus} + \alpha_3 \text{ Research} + \alpha_4 \text{ Age} + \alpha_5 \text{ Status} + \varepsilon_i$$

Overall Score$_{it}$
$$= \alpha_0 + \alpha_1 \text{ Size} + \alpha_2 \text{ Focus} + \alpha_3 \text{ Research} + \alpha_4 \text{ Age} + \alpha_5 \text{ Status} + \varepsilon_i$$

Overall Score$_{it}$ = α_0 + α_1 Academic Reputation Rank + α_2 Employer Reputation Rank + α_3 Faculty Student Rank + α_4 Citations per Faculty Rank + α_5 International Faculty Rank + α_6 International Student Rank + ε_i

Likewise, it also models individual institution unobserved effect as:

Overall Score$_{it}$ = α_0 + α_1 Academic Reputation Rank$_{it}$ + α_2 Employer Reputation Rank$_{it}$ + α_3 Faculty Student Rank$_{it}$ + α_4 Citations per Faculty Rank$_{it}$ + α_5 International Faculty Rank$_{it}$ + α_6 International Student Rank$_{it}$ + ε_{it}

(t = 1, 2, 3 ... T)

Therefore,

Overall Score$_{it}$ = α_0 + α_1 Academic Reputation Rank$_{it}$ + α_2 Employer Reputation Rank$_{it}$ + α_3 Faculty Student Rank$_{it}$ + α_4 Citations per Faculty Rank$_{it}$ + α_5 International Faculty Rank$_{it}$ + α_6 International Student Rank$_{it}$ + ε_{it}

The analysis assumed that the overall score is likely influenced by a factor outside the explanatory variables, while the regressors varied over time. The fixed-random effect and the Hausman test are suitable in the analysis. The next model is a corollary of the above model.

So, the analysis used fixed and random effect techniques to consider the effect of unobserved individual institution-specific characteristics. Interestingly, 61% of the universities captured for analysis are private institutions. Though the data are normally distributed, i.e., 95% of the size dataset is within normal distribution, the academic reputation rank dataset represents an unequal distribution. There is a little tail on the right but no tail on the left side of the distribution. However, academic reputation score dataset still represent the normal distribution without the right and left tails. The 'focus' dataset represents the unequal distribution, where the data is low toward the lower figure, increasing more at the average. Moreover, the 'employer reputable rank' dataset skewed toward the right of the distribution. The 'faculty-student score' dataset represents normal distribution without both left and right tails, whereas the 'faculty-student rank' dataset represents the right-skewed distribution. 'Citation per faculty score' dataset represents the distribution of the data. Results show that there is a distribution toward the right of the dataset. The 'international faculty score', 'faculty rank', and 'international student score' datasets all represent the data distribution. Finally, the overall score/ranking dataset represents the distribution of the data.

Figure 1 shows that many participating institutions (42%) belong to the 'Large' category. Though institution 'size' can be misleading (see Shin & Toutkoushian, 2011; Olcay & Bulu, 2017), it indicates institutions' capacity to accommodate many academic programs, professors, infrastructure, and the resources available to manage them. Simply put, many institutions on the top 100 universities table of QS ranking in Asia can be categorized as 'Large'. This size may have also contributed to their ability to meet QS indicators, ultimately ranking them as 'world-class' universities. Resources are crucial and can be a determining factor for the size of the institutions. Therefore, the ample availability of resources and its sound management could be an advantage in meeting ranking criteria. However, whether institution size and good ranking make a considerable impact in society is yet to be determined. Suppose ranking indicators could include social impact and sustainable development in their criteria. In that case, the size effect may even help Asia and institutions' reputable status may assist in resolving several social issues present in the region.

Similarly, many of the institutions (54%), as shown in Figure 2, have fully comprehensive academic programs, which probably gives them an advantage

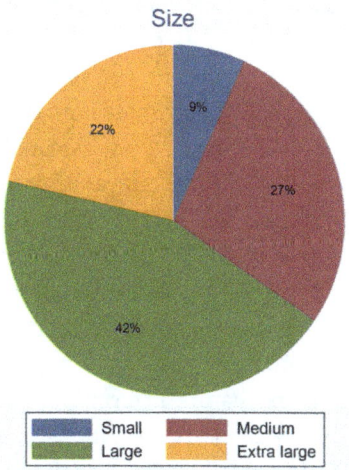

FIGURE 1   Classification according to institutions' size

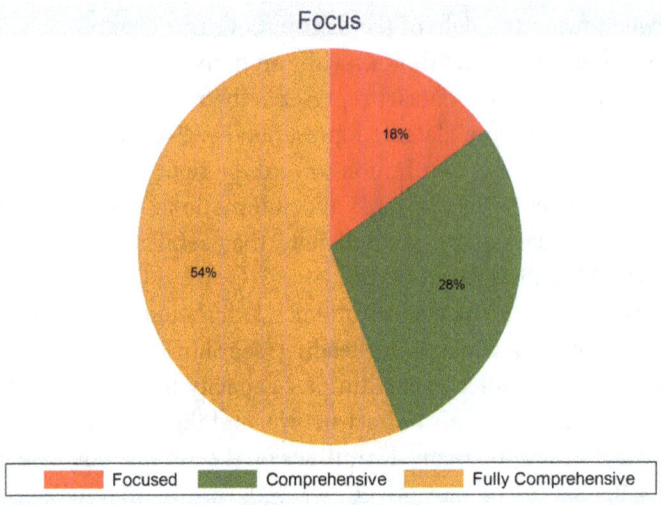

FIGURE 2   The focus of institutions

in terms of research outputs and revenue generation (see Marginson, 2014). It should also be highlighted that many of these Asian institutions also fall under the 'Large' category.

Therefore, data indicates that the 100 world-class universities ranked by QS are the largest and most comprehensive universities in Asia. These findings illustrate the significance of having access and the opportunity to use resources to meet performance indicators of World University Rankings. Also, the majority of the institutions (82%), as shown in Figure 3, have a very high performance in research. According to QS indicators, this means they can produce many publications with high citations per faculty.

This performance may be linked to the availability of resources in these institutions, as depicted by their size and ability to operate at full capacity. It can, therefore, be concluded that there is a link between size, institution focus, and ability to perform well in research. Still, QS indicators do not elaborate on the type of research (see Larivière & Gingras, 2014) assessed and whether knowledge through these publications is of local relevance or just promoting global knowledge based on rankings' criteria. Therefore, the omission of such details prevents us from affirming that quality is determined by the number of publications or institution size. Moreover, it cannot be confirmed whether these institutions provide quality or have an impact on their society despite their comprehensive academic programs.

In Figure 4, 36% of the institutions are 'mature' in terms of years of establishment. Historically, all institutions on the top 100 QS are more than 50 years old.

Hence, institutions' age and longevity might indicate their experience managing higher education Institutions and ensuring academic programs' sustainability and continuity.

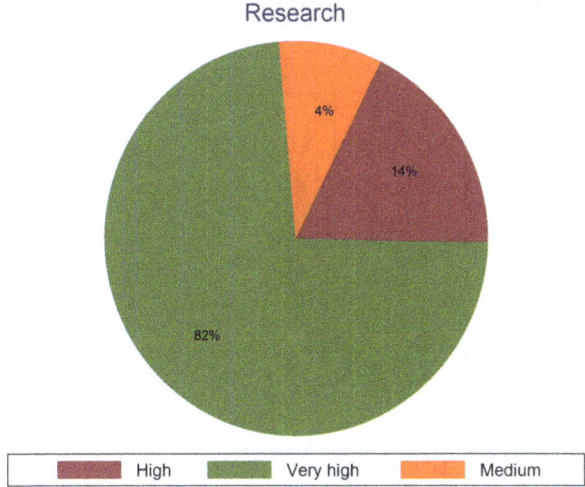

FIGURE 3   The research of institutions

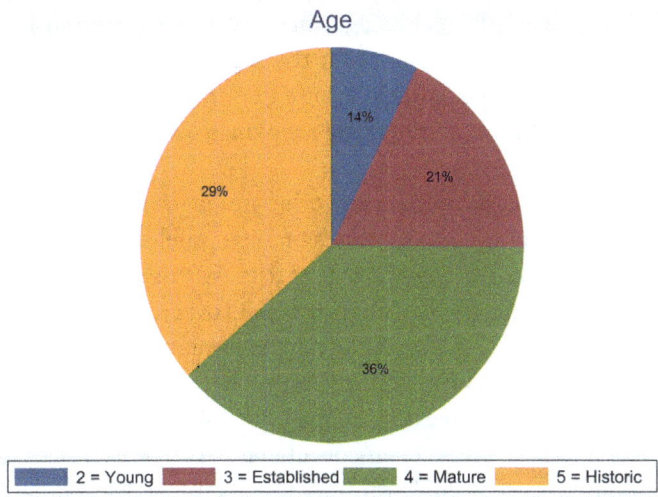

FIGURE 4   The age of institutions: 5 = Historic (more than 100 years old institutions); 4 = Mature (50 to 100 years old institutions); 3 = Established (25 to 50 years old institutions); 2 = Young (10 to 25 years old institutions)

In Figure 5, most institutions that have performed well or are in the top 100 of the QS rankings are private institutions. This is an interesting finding for Asia, as it shows that the region could have many private institutions offering higher education products. These private sectors have experienced and committed to meeting ranking's quality criteria, which has led to reputation improvement. Presuming the majority of quality higher education institutions in Asia are

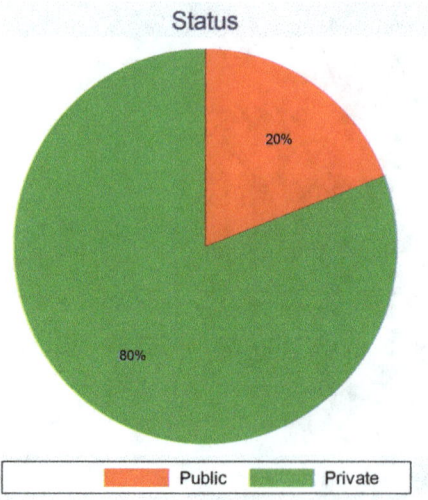

FIGURE 5   The status of institutions, whether public or private

private, this finding is important as the private sector can help governments advance research in science and technology that can eventually translate to innovation that will create development for the region. Similarly, public-private partnerships may also be needed to ensure that the impact of private institutions enjoying a good reputation through ranking can be used to provide solutions to several social issues.

Aside from institutions' classification, many other problems are associated with ranking and its methodology. The solutions to these problems are deeply rooted in understanding trends through historical data. With this, one of the most important concerns should be the behavior of data over a certain period and across QS ranking indicators used in ranking to determine future implications for both universities and society.

The present century is characterized by changes disrupting higher education's operation, which may not have been considered when global rankings and criteria were initially introduced. For instance, one critical disruption or change is a worldwide drift toward the digital transformation that has changed how research is conducted; teaching is imparted and offered programs. Digital transformation has also changed the methods used to ensure institutional quality and improvement. Therefore, the analysis of QS panel data from different years will be helpful not only to assist us in understanding the implications of the methodology used in ranking but also in using ranking results differently. If we apply Plato's philosophy to rankings, rankers then may have to consider that every university and country is unique. Besides, it is hardly plausible to believe that the process of ranking universities has a reputational effect that benefits every member of society.

In most cases, ranking only benefits the elite. Therefore, what is left is for us to discover what the data can reveal about the occurrences or fluctuations over time and how this discovery could influence the QS design and evaluation metrics, for example. The analysis further considers reports published by the QS in 2012, 2013, 2016, 2018 and 2020 to reflect on critical issues of social justice and Plato's views of a just society. In this case, the analysis considers six metrics: academic reputation, employer reputation, faculty/student ratio, citation per faculty, international faculty ratio and QS international ratio.

The analysis aims to observe the commonality or changes in the data over a selected period based on these metrics.

3   Academic Reputation

QS assigns 40% of the total weighting to academic reputation score (Huang, 2012). This metric is assessed based on responses from over 130,000 expert opinions invited to evaluate institutions (Laura, 2022). This index usually seeks answers from experts about the quality of universities. The criteria may allow universities' alumni with solid networks to dominate the survey and give positive ratings to the universities with which they are or were affiliated. Though preventing such bias entirely is unachievable, this particular index has ignited debates and has been profoundly challenged in the literature. Hence, it is necessary to identify emerging trends in the evaluation pattern over time and determine the ramifications of allocating the highest weighting in the QS ranking methodology framework to academic reputation. It should be acknowledged that should the invited experts or evaluators be from institutions and publication databases, respondents from universities that control the editorial board of journals are likely to be selected. While QS policy does not allow evaluators to choose the institutions of their affiliation, it does not prevent the evaluating elite alumni from considering that elite Western universities may deserve a nomination for reputation rankings. Likewise, according to QS, evaluators' geographical location at the time of evaluation may not necessarily be their home university or one with which they have previous connections. With this policy, QS rankings have mentioned how they intend to eliminate biases that could arise in their analyses.

Similarly, QS considers respondents' location and affiliation and disallows self-nominations, among others, in determining the eligibility of evaluators (Laura, 2022). On the other hand, the implication of these policies on the credibility of ranking results should be clarified. For instance, Table 5 gives an account of the academic reputation ranking of institutions from different years in Asia.

TABLE 5 Pairwise correlations of institutions' academic reputation

Variables	(1)	(2)	(3)	(4)	(5)	(6)
Academic reputation	1.000					
Size	−0.208	1.000				
Focus	−0.286	0.565	1.000			
Research	−0.172	−0.077	−0.076	1.000		
Age	−0.251	0.368	0.311	0.050	1.000	
Status	−0.117	0.121	0.009	0.097	−0.077	1.000

3.1 Pairwise Correlations of Institutions' Academic Reputation

Table 5 shows that the *size, status, focus, research increases, and age* negatively correlate with academic reputation. Firstly, the negative correlation with academic reputation suggests that research, size and focus are correlated. Interpreting these results shows that ranking improves institutions' reputation, but the size of institutions is insignificant to maintain this ranking in the future. In Asian institutions, size could refer to how large or small the academic faculties are in terms of the number of programs offered. Basically, small institutions with quality academic programs may be able to have sustainable academic quality. Likewise, the age classification of institutions becomes irrelevant in achieving 'world-class' status or reputation when institutions have achieved good status, good academic focus and are productive in terms of research publications. It means the oldest institutions have not become reputable in their academic focus, and that focus and research may have declined at a particular time.

Secondly, institutions' age and research are correlated. Essentially, the size and age of an institution may not necessarily be used to achieve rankings in the long run. A few large and older institutions may be experiencing challenges because of their emphasis on institution size and history rather than on factors affecting reputation, which ultimately translates to a good ranking in QS evaluation metrics.

4   Employer Reputation

The QS metric to measure employers' views of universities' academic performance and whether they produce work-ready graduates is weighted at 10% on average and relies on over 75,000 responses from employers of graduates (Laura, 2022). These criteria may benefit universities with many undergraduate programs or comprehensive programs because their size facilitates the production of many graduates yearly. According to QS policy (Laura, 2022), employers may only nominate 10 institutions they presume to have produced employable graduates. Likewise, they can nominate 30 institutions outside their region that they believe in having produced the best graduates. Depending on the dominant industry, employers' preferences regarding what their organization considers employable graduates are likely to influence their selections and might not necessarily be based on the quality of the academic curriculum. However, QS has measures to eliminate biases in the analysis and calculation to determine the universities with the best reputation according to employers in terms of graduate employability (see Laura, 2022). Table 6 provides details of the analysis of employment rank criteria for the QS metric.

4.1 Regression of Size, Focus, Research, Age, Status, and Log of Academic Reputation Rank of Institutions

Table 6 shows that *size, status, focus, research,* and *age* negatively correlate with academic reputation. The negative correlation indicates that *research, size,* and *focus* are correlated. Graduates' employment opportunities or the ability to attract prospective employers are not predetermined by institutions' *age* and *size* classification. On the other hand, the increase in institutions' status due to a rise in ranking reputation might positively influence their ability to increase in size in terms of infrastructure, academic programs offered and the number of research publications. This correlation between *status, size,* and *research* explicate why many Asian institutions continue to make the rankings list regardless of the age classification. However, as institutions' ranking improves reputation, the relevance of increased academic offerings and research should be seen as facilitators in promoting development in the region. 'Development promoters' should include research and programs that sustain national cultural identity. In other words, *status* could be used to preserve endangered cultures and history in some Asian countries.

TABLE 6   Pairwise correlation of employment rank

Variables	(1)	(2)	(3)	(4)	(5)	(6)
Employment rank	1.000					
Size	−0.298	1.000				
Focus	−0.283	0.565	1.000			
Research	−0.172	−0.063	−0.075	1.000		
Age	−0.254	0.374	0.311	0.057	1.000	
Status	−0.053	0.128	0.026	0.142	−0.052	1.000

TABLE 7 Institutional characteristics and employer reputation rank

Variables	OLS employer reputation rank[a]
Size	−0.196**
	(0.0785)
Focus	−0.0759
	(0.0822)
Research	−0.340***
	(0.0827)
Age	−0.270***
	(0.0580)
Status	0.00994
	(0.110)
Constant	7.208***
	(0.334)
Observations	342
R-squared	0.192

***p < 0.01, **p < 0.05, * p < 0.1
a   Standard errors in parentheses.

Table 7 shows which of the institutions' categories predicts employer rank or influences employer choice of institutions, graduates or programs.

4.2   Regression of Size, Focus, Research, Age, Status and Log of Employer Reputation Rank

Table 7 estimates the *size, focus, research, age* and *status* on the Employment Rank using ordinary least squares (OLS). Findings show that the institutional characteristics negatively correlate with graduate employability. Variables such as *size, research,* and *age* have a significant negative association with employment rank. In other words, *size, research, age* of institutions and graduates' employability are not related. The employment opportunities for graduates lie in quality teaching and curriculum relevance to a country's development, which is often not emphasized in ranking indicators. *Focus* has a negative but insignificant relationship with the dependent variable. Thus, the academic focus of an institution does not necessarily predict success or failure on the job market. Meanwhile, *status* has a positive but insignificant relationship with the employability. This finding shows that the reputation of institutions could contribute to better or more graduate employment opportunities in Asia.

5 Faculty/Student Ratio

The quality of teaching and learning is a metric in QS ranking and is weighted at 20% (Laura, 2022). This criterion is judged by students' experiences of the curriculum and the support provided by their institutions. Essentially, it tries to understand institutions' staffing systems in terms of the potential influence of the faculty-student ratio on the quality of teaching and support. The QS yearly report provides a rating for universities performing well in this category. However, this performance trend needs further analysis of the evaluated institutions' size, focus, size, and the research over a given period. Globally, universities are adopting austerity measures regarding recruitment and opting for part-time appointments to provide teaching and support to students. Alas, these measures are detrimental to the most vulnerable staff's academic careers who seek tenures or permanent positions. It is unlikely that the QS report or analysis can show these dynamics. However, changes in data behavior could tell us whether optimal performance in teaching can be attributed to institutions' good ethical practices or to other factors that could have implications for the quality and future of Higher Education in Asia. Table 8 demonstrates how the student-faculty ratio changes the dynamic of ranking assessment for QS over time.

5.1 *Pairwise Correlation of Faculty-Student Ranking*

Table 8 shows that *focus* and *research* negatively correlate with faculty-student ranking. The negative correlation between these variables (focus and research) and faculty-student ranking suggests that *size*, *age*, and *status* positively correlate

TABLE 8 Pairwise correlation of faculty-student ranking

Variables	(1)	(2)	(3)	(4)	(5)	(6)
Employment rank	1.000					
Size	−0.180	1.000				
Focus	−0.063	0.565	1.000			
Research	−0.044	−0.064	−0.075	1.000		
Age	−0.004	0.373	0.311	0.057	1.000	
Status	−0.015	0.128	0.026	0.142	−0.052	1.000

with faculty-student ranking. Also, *age* and *status* increase as faculty-student ranking increases, whereas *focus* and *research* decrease. These results demonstrate that the age and status of public or private institutions contribute to effective teaching and learning when considering the faculty-student ratio. Meanwhile, the focus of the institutions and the ability to do research are affected by faculty-student ranking. In this case, workload impacts academics responsible for teaching and research. How the institution distributes work or what the emphasis is placed on determines whether teaching and/or research are affected, which would subsequently impact their scores in rankings. Likewise, Table 9 predicts which of the institutions' categories help improve teaching and student satisfaction in Asian institutions.

5.2 Regression of Size, Focus, Research, Age, Status, and Log of Faculty Student Rank

Table 9 presents the estimation of *size, focus, research, age,* and *status* on the Faculty Student Rank using ordinary least squares (OLS). *Size* has a significant positive relationship with faculty-student rank, while *focus* has a significant negative relationship with faculty-student rank. Also, *age* has a negative and significant

TABLE 9　Institutional characteristics and faculty student rank

Variables	Log of faculty student rank[a]
Size	0.385***
	(0.0534)
Focus	−0.188***
	(0.0573)
Research	−0.102
	(0.0624)
Age	−0.0732*
	(0.0426)
Status	−0.130
	(0.0906)
Constant	5.493***
	(0.262)
Observations	424
R-squared	0.119

***$p < 0.01$, **$p < 0.05$, *$p < 0.1$
a Standard errors in parentheses.

association with faculty-student rank. *Status* has an insignificant negative relationship with the dependent variable (reputation rankings). The result points to the fact that only the *focus* of institutions influenced the faculty-student ratio.

It should be noted that institutions' *focus* is an aspect of teaching and learning. Thus, students learning experience depends on the program departments, whether an institution is research-intensive, and their years of experience, i.e., how long they have been in existence. Meanwhile, *status* cannot determine learning experience because it depends on factors such as the *focus*, *research* and *age* of institutions. In other words, ranking reputation alone cannot contribute to quality teaching and learning or faculty-student ratio. However, *age* negatively affects the faculty-student score, but not significantly, which implies that not all traditional universities are at the top-ranked level. However, Table 10 shows a different perspective on internationalization based on International Students Rank and its determinants.

5.3 Regression of Size, Focus, Research, Age, Status and Log of International Students Rank

Table 10 presents the estimation of *size*, *focus*, *research*, *age* and *status* on the International Students Rank using ordinary least squares (OLS). Variables such

TABLE 10 Institutional characteristics and International Students Rank

Variables	International Students Rank[a]
Size	0.226***
	(0.0853)
Focus	−0.408***
	(0.0841)
Research	0.190*
	(0.101)
Age	0.404***
	(0.0634)
Status	0.132
	(0.140)
Constant	4.007***
	(0.387)
Observations	269
R-squared	0.245

***$p < 0.01$, **$p < 0.05$, *$p < 0.1$
a Standard errors in parentheses.

as *size*, *age*, and *research* all have a significant positive association with International Students Rank. In contrast, *focus* has a significant negative relationship with the dependent variable. Though *status* also has a negative relationship with the dependent variable, it is not substantial. Results show international students' growth in the evaluated institutions based on *size*, *age* and *research*. These findings depict that older institutions with comprehensive programs and a remarkable ability to conduct research and produce outputs are likely to be well ranked and attract international students. Interestingly, the institutional *focus* on programs offered did not influence rankings or international students' mobility to those institutions.

6   Citations per Faculty

Institutions' research output is an indication of several realities. Firstly, it shows evidence of access to resources necessary to recruit qualified academics equipped to produce research worthy of international recognition, as per Elsevier's Scopus database (Laura, 2022). The QS system calculates institutions' citation per faculty publication metrics over five years to give a ranking in this category. Ample disapproving remarks have emerged in existing literature for rankers' failure to consider the advantage that this criterion could give to predominantly science-based institutions (see Sowter, Reggio, & Hijazi, 2017). In terms of research outputs, critics find that this category may disadvantage humanities or social sciences-based institutions or academics. Science academics tend to produce more research than others due to the availability of journals and the nature of their work, which is different from their counterparts in other fields. As of 2015, QS adopted different measurements to ensure that research citations do not constitute a disadvantage for those in the non-life sciences (Laura, 2022). Evidently, one of the ways to reduce bias is for the QS system not to consider self-citations. Table 11 illustrates the relationship between academic staff citations and other categories.

6.1   *Pairwise Correlation of Citations Per Faculty*

Results in Table 11 indicate that as *citation ranking* increases by one unit *size* and *focus* increase to 20.2% and 25.8% respectively. Since *research* and *age* decrease as *citation ranking* increases, the number of an institution's research publications and its age can neither determine *citation per faculty* nor the quality of its research outputs. As such, rankings indicators need to reflect on how to better assess institutions' research performance beyond the number of publications or citations that a faculty can accumulate.

TABLE 11   Pairwise correlation of citations per faculty

Variables	(1)	(2)	(3)	(4)	(5)	(6)
Citation ranking	1.000					
Size	0.202	1.000				
Focus	0.258	0.565	1.000			
Research	−0.172	−0.064	−0.075	1.000		
Age	0.005	0.373	0.311	0.057	1.000	
Status	−0.158	0.128	0.026	0.142	−0.052	1.000

7   International Faculty/International Student Ratio

The international faculty and international student ratios are given only 5% each of the total weighting (Laura, 2022). These criteria allow institutions to demonstrate their ability to attract international faculty and international students. The rank obtained in this category is likely to be influenced by other metrics such as *reputation* and institutions' *research* performance. These metrics promote institutions to the international community, such as students who require quality education outside their country of origin and foreign academics looking for research collaboration or institutional partnership. One would expect the weighting for these categories to be more than 5%, though other influential factors are also linked to performance in internationalization.

Nevertheless, it is imperative to understand international students and academic mobility patterns over a period of time to determine whether other

TABLE 12   Pairwise correlation of international faculty score

Variables	(1)	(2)	(3)	(4)	(5)	(6)
Score	1.000					
Size	0.0141	1.000				
Focus	0.1988	0.5648	1.000			
Research	0.638	−0.635	−0.074	1.000		
Age	−0.1033	0.3725	0.3108	0.0567	1.000	
Status	−0.1226	0.1226	0.055	0.1416	−0.052	1.000

factors could have influenced the ratios or brought about a level of change. Data collection on students and faculty for these categories is based on data from government agencies in different countries. Sourcing information from official structures demonstrates that data accuracy is essential to understanding what has happened for a certain period.

7.1 Pairwise Correlation of International Faculty Score

A unit increase in *International Faculty Score* leads to an increase in *size* (1.4%), *focus* (19.9%), and *research* (6.4%). In other words, *size*, *focus*, and *research* positively correlate with *International Students Score*. A unit increase in *International Faculty Score* leads to an increase in *size* (1.4%), *focus* (19.9%), and *research* (6.4%). As *age* (10.3%) and *status* (12.3%) decrease, the *International Students Score* increases. It also means that a unit increase in *International Students Rank* yields an increase in *size* (19.7%), *research* (23.2%), *age* (38.72%) and *status* (7.2%). These results establish that private or public institutional *status* neither determines the level of international partnership and collaboration nor the number of international academics in the institutions. However, an institution's age has a more significant influence on its internationalization capacity than *size, focus* and *research ability*. It can be deduced that the academic *reputation* score is determined by an institution's profile, non-inclusive of *size* and *focus*. Simply put, institutions' *size* and *focus* will not influence a faculty's ability to be productive in terms of research publications, nor will it contribute to their *reputation* ranking. Table 13 indicates the determining factors enabling institutions to attract international faculty.

7.2 Regression of Size, Focus, Research, Age, Status, and Log of International Faculty Rank

Table 13 presents the estimation of *size, focus, research, age* and *status* on the International Faculty Rank using ordinary least squares (OLS). Variables such as *focus* and *status* have a negative and significant association with International Faculty Rank, whereas *size, research* and *age* have a positive and significant association with the dependent variable. In sum, *size, research* and institution *age* constitute the elements facilitating institutions' ability to attract international faculty or researchers who may contribute to an increase in research outputs and citations. Therefore, the largest and oldest institutions with research capacity are better positioned to meet QS ranking indicators' internationalization criteria. *Size* and *focus* have a significant positive association with *International Faculty Score*, whereas *age* and *status* have a negative and considerable relationship with the dependent variable.

TABLE 13   Institutional characteristics and International Faculty Rank

Variables	OLS International Faculty Rank[a]
Size	0.243**
	(0.103)
Focus	−0.330***
	(0.108)
Research	0.282**
	(0.111)
Age	0.588***
	(0.0784)
Status	−0.380**
	(0.179)
Constant	3.417***
	(0.456)
Observations	320
R-squared	0.246

***$p < 0.01$, **$p < 0.05$, *$p < 0.1$
a   Standard errors in parentheses.

Moreover, *research* also has a negative relationship with the dependent variable. Hence, we can conclude that productivity in terms of an institution's ability to produce research will not include their *reputation* score nor serve as an indicator for international students. Put differently, international students may not necessarily consider the research output of institutions or interpret research ability/capacity as motivation when choosing an institution to attend.

The results in Table 14 differ for international students, as shown in Table 13.

7.3   *Regression of Size, Focus, Research, Age, Status, and Log of International Students Score*

Table 14 presents the estimation of *size, focus, research, age* and *status* on the International Students Score using ordinary least squares (OLS). Variables such as *focus* and *research* have a positive and significant association with *International Students Score*. While *age* and *status* have a significant negative relationship with the international students score, focus decreases as international

TABLE 14 Institutional characteristics and International Students Score

Variables	Log International Students Score[a]
Size	−0.0657
	(0.0722)
Focus	0.447***
	(0.0746)
Research	0.229***
	(0.0794)
Age	−0.250***
	(0.0582)
Status	−0.403***
	(0.126)
Constant	3.094***
	(0.355)
Observations	562
R-squared	0.100

***p < 0.01, **p < 0.05, *p < 0.1
a Standard errors in parentheses.

student rank increases. The result means *size, research,* and *age* contributed to high outcomes in international student indicator ranking scores, whilst the focus of programs did not result in international student ranking scores. In this case, international students' profiles did not necessarily determine rank or cause improvements in institutions' *age, status, and research* for reputation or ranking.

7.4   *Regression, Size, Focus, Research, Age, Status and Log of the Overall Score*

Table 15 presents the estimation of *size, focus, research, age* and *status* on the overall score using ordinary least squares (OLS). Variables such as *focus, research, age* and *status* have a positive and important association with overall score. Yet, the *size* variable has a negative relationship with the dependent variable, which is insignificant. It can, therefore, be concluded that the overall determinants of reputation ranking for institutions are the focus of programs, the ability to conduct and produce quality research, age and whether the institutions are private or public.

TABLE 15 Institutional characteristics and log of the overall score

Variables	Overall score[a]
Size	−0.0158
	(0.0216)
Focus	0.155***
	(0.0222)
Research	0.213***
	(0.0241)
Age	0.0560***
	(0.0172)
Status	0.0771**
	(0.0374)
Constant	2.667***
	(0.105)
Observations	538
R-squared	0.250

***$p < 0.01$, **$p < 0.05$, *$p < 0.1$
a Standard errors in parentheses.

8 Conclusion

The focus on ranking in Asia serves to advance the debate on social justice and contribute to the discourse on the purpose of global university ranking. The analysis of QS World university metrics and data foregrounds important dynamics, including how institutions' characteristics have influenced rankings metrics over the years. Though the numbers did not reveal much about the critical issue of social justice and development in Asia, they offered a new lens through which we could analyze issues surrounding the QS ranking system. It provided a unique perspective on the complexity of metrics, the challenges associated with the evaluation and methodology of ranking universities that are profoundly different historically, culturally, and in terms of access to resources, as well as education rights and politics of social justice. The framing helped analyze and discuss social justice to include the essential role that rankings may play in promoting social justice in Asia and elsewhere.

Asia should therefore consider rankings as a policy opportunity to promote nation-building. The concept of nation-building obscured the realities of ethnonationalism (see Olcay & Bulu, 2017), which was submerged by the overarching monolithic ideology of communism (see Rothbard, 1979) in the former Soviet Union and Eastern Europe (Selverstone, 2009). This ideology manifested in different forms in Asia. It is hoped that QS metrics and QS criteria can help participating institutions create a cultural identity informally through socialization in a given ethnocultural milieu and formally through ranking outcomes.

References

Anowar, F., Helal, M. A., Afroj, S., Sultana, S., Sarker, F., & Mamun, K. A. (2015). A critical review on world university ranking in terms of top four ranking systems. In K. Elleithy & T. Sobh (Eds.), *New trends in networking, computing, e-learning, systems sciences, and engineering* (pp. 559–566). Springer. https://doi.org/10.1007/978-3-319-06764-3_72

Berbegal-Mirabent, J., & Ribeiro-Soriano, D. E. (2015). Behind league tables and ranking systems: A critical perspective of how university quality is measured. *Journal of Service Theory and Practice*.

Gaure, S. (2013). OLS with multiple high dimensional category variables. *Computational Statistics & Data Analysis, 66*, 8–18.

Hayes, A. F., & Cai, L. (2007). Using heteroskedasticity-consistent standard error estimators in OLS regression: An introduction and software implementation. *Behavior Research Methods, 39*(4), 709–722.

Huang, M. H. (2012). Opening the black box of QS world university rankings. *Research Evaluation, 21*(1), 71–78.

Larivière, V., & Gingras, Y. (2014). 10 Measuring interdisciplinarity. In B. Cronin & C. Sugimoto (Eds.), *Beyond bibliometrics: Harnessing multidimensional indicators of scholarly impact* (p. 187). The MIT Press.

Laura, L. (2022). *QS World University Rankings methodology: Using rankings to start your university search*. Retrieved June 12, 2022, from https://www.topuniversities.com/qs-world-university-rankings/methodology

Lee, J., Liu, K., & Wu, Y. (2020). Does the Asian catch-up model of world-class universities work? Revisiting the zero-sum game of global university rankings and government policies. *Educational Research for Policy and Practice, 19*(3), 319–343.

Marginson, S. (2014). University rankings and social science. *European Journal of Education, 49*(1), 45–59.

Olcay, G. A., & Bulu, M. (2017). Is measuring the knowledge creation of universities possible? A review of university rankings. *Technological Forecasting and Social Change, 123*, 153–160.

Rothbard, M. N. (1979). The myth of monolithic communism. *Libertarian Review, 8*(1), 32–35.

Schulze-Cleven, T., Reitz, T., Maesse, J., & Angermuller, J. (2017). The new political economy of higher education: Between distributional conflicts and discursive stratification. *Higher Education, 73*(6), 795–812.

Selverstone, M. J. (2009). *Constructing the monolith: The United States, Great Britain, and international communism, 1945–1950*. Harvard University Press.

Shin, J. C., & Toutkoushian, R. K. (2011). The past, present, and future of university rankings. In J. Shin, R. Toutkoushian, & U. Teichler (Eds.), *University rankings* (pp. 1–16). Springer. https://doi.org/10.1007/978-94-007-1116-7_1

Sowter, B., Reggio, D., & Hijazi, S. (2017). QS world university rankings. In B. Sowter, D. Reggio, & S. Hijazi (Eds.), *Research analytics* (pp. 121–136). Auerbach Publications.

Van Bruinessen, M. (2011). *Kurdish ethno-nationalism versus nation-building states*. Gorgias Press.

CHAPTER 3

Critiquing Ranking Methods

Abstract

The university rankings methodology has been criticized for its subjective nature (Debrota, 2016; Huang, 2012). On the other hand, this chapter critiques the peer-review process involved in determining world-class universities in ranking systems. The focus is on the transparency and statistical explanation of instruments used in calculating Asian universities' performance. The critique includes how ranking methodologies may mislead in determining the performance of higher education institutions. Moreover, the statistics used to estimate and forecast higher education performance were explained and analyzed in this case. This chapter offers a discussion on how ranking agencies use various statistics to determine the best 100 universities. Primarily, the chapter argues that ranking organizations need to validate the peer-review process and source of data to have a holistic view of higher education performance in Asia. The advantage of applying multiple data sources is that it allows fairness and could improve confidence in ranking results. Therefore, this chapter concludes that statistical designs that give an advantage to historically well-resourced universities should be avoided to improve confidence in global university rankings.

Keywords

ranking scores – indicators – quantitative methods – statistics – higher education – Asia

1 Introduction

The use of quantitative methods to assess outcomes is not new and can be traced as far back as early human history (Creswell & Clark, 2007, p. 388). The emergence of the industrial revolution in the 1880s encouraged researchers in science to use statistical and scientific management tools in making complex decisions (Ozcan, 2005). Quantifying outcomes is based on the assumption that it provides a reliable comparison in ranking results and ratings (Tarlow, Brossart, McCammon, Giovanetti, Belle, & Philip, 2021). Put differently, it is possible to ensure the objectivity of ranking or factors used in ranking universities if the evaluation is done objectively and correctly. In terms of university rankings, the quantitative approach has been used by rating agencies on different performance indicators (Mahassen, 2014). Likewise, the assumption is that the quantitative approach could provide reliable scores that may be used to make strategic decisions by the university leaders (Uslu, 2020). Despite improvement in THE and QS methodologies (Sowter, 2008), data collection errors remain a challenge in the Asian higher education ranking process (Fauzi, Tan, Daud, & Awalludin, 2020). These errors could yield inauspicious ranking outputs and subsequently mislead policy if undetected. This chapter aims to provide a clear understanding of quantitative methods used in global university rankings, focusing on QS ranking design and methods. The purpose is to explain how quantitative methods and statistical tools can be improved for ranking systems.

The quantitative method is considered an objective technique to measure university performance based on a set of indicators (Rodriguez, Saiz, & Bas, 2009; Katharaki & Katharakis, 2010). Generally, it sometimes means using symbols, numberings, mathematical explanations, and other features of quantifications useful in assisting decision-makers in arriving at a systematic and validated judgment (Zikmund, Babin, Carr, & Griffin, 2013, p. XVIII). Asian universities require improvement in the ability and capacity to deliver Quality, particularly in the Southeast Asian region (Hallinger, 2010). So, rankings for Asian universities may either offer an opportunity to detect areas in need of improvement or could create confusion for governance if scoring contains methodological errors. In any case, reliably conducting ranking processes may explain how low-performing universities in Asia can improve.

Based on the criteria of most influential institution ranking bodies (see Figure 6), the QS ranking indicators put the highest percentages on academic reputation or academic peer review (40%) (see Anowar, Helal, Afroj, Sultana, Sarker, & Mamun, 2015). Nonetheless, further justification is required to understand the implications of the weighting for evaluating higher education performance.

Likewise, other indicators such as faculty-student ratios and citations per faculty are weighted at 20%. The indicators are considered necessary after academic peer-review, which means that academic peer-review and research take 60% of QS review indicators. Employer's reputation indicator counts 10%, while international students and international faculty make up 5%. It should be noted that international faculty still forms part of the research ability of the universities. Both the international student indicator and employer reputation are linked because universities' alumni provide the basis for employers' feedback.

In summary, QS ranking indicators focus heavily on peer-review based on the university's ability to produce internationally recognized research. Yet, it is not

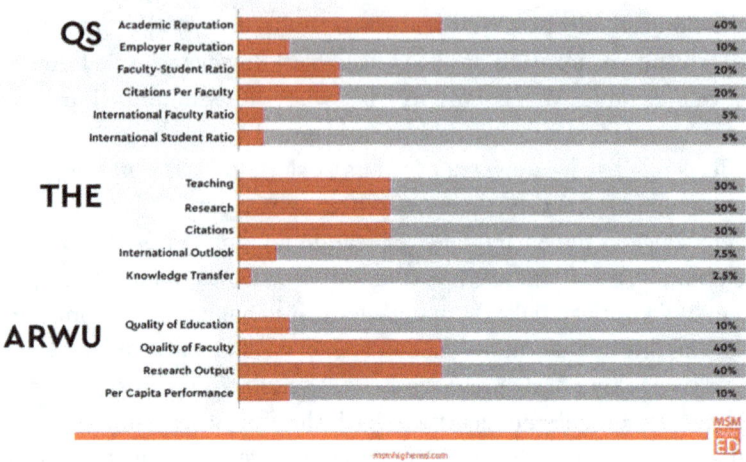

FIGURE 6   Criteria of most influential institution ranking bodies
SOURCE: HTTPS://MSMHIGHERED.COM/INSIGHTS-POST/IMPORTANCE-OF-UNIVERSITY-RANKINGS-FOR-INSTITUTIONS/

clear why different metrics and/or weighing systems are used to determine the research performance of Asian universities. A process where QS allows respondents to nominate universities for ranking during a survey may be prone to bias and unfair to universities with low international connections. Peer review, as a weighty indicator in the ranking system, will always favor universities with a strong alumni network worldwide.

The summary of QS evaluation of universities in Asia has been described with metaphors like "ride a tiger" (Jeremic & Jovanovic-Milenkovic, 2014) or risky competition. However, the increase in participating Asian universities shows their level of readiness to compete. It means that it is causing serious but unequal competition in Asia because of the assumption made on indicators to rank their universities (Chan, 2012). Yet, the user of ranking reports expects fairness and transparency. For instance, statistical techniques such as the Pareto chart representing ranking figures helped evaluate higher education in the Gulf area (Al-Bashir, 2016). Still, its applicability in global ranking depends on the data utilized. Generally, the mean value is calculated on a ranking table or a chart based on survey outcomes on different indicators to determine the rank of the top best universities (Moed, 2017). The mean value in ranking represents the average score of the total observation of the institutions against each indicator. Therefore, selecting respondents who score each indicator should not be biased to ensure the objectivity of ranking. So, measuring Asian universities along with the rest of the universities based on this method means objectivity is followed in sampling and attribution of ranks.

Most users of ranking results usually see computed descriptive statistics that show the first top ten and best 100 in relation to ranking criteria. They might not be aware of the intricacies of sampling and determining the mean value that resulted in selecting the best universities.

The first thing to analyze in the ranking of top-performing institutions is to 'exterminate' the top ten top institutions to know what determines their position in the top ten rankings. The ranking charts also provide glance information about top-performing institutions and units of measurement. Another statistic to look for is the percentages, as it shows the difference between top-ranked and low-ranked universities or changes in global rankings over time. The percentage of Asian universities in QS universities has increased since 2020. Though the rate shows improvement in ranking, they do not indicate the factors responsible for this improvement. In addition, it doesn't show how universities outside East Asia can improve their Quality. It is unlikely that few ranked universities in Asia can provide change and development in knowledge production for the continent. Therefore, Asia must calculate changes or differences in ranking scores and create a process to address these issues, not just attempting the race of "ride the tiger".

While the methodology of ranking is problematic, specific statistics allow the analysis of the changes in higher education systems. To that effect, the Fishbone diagram is a simple problem-analysis tool that can analyze education outcomes (Atchuthan & Elangkumaran, 2021), including possible solutions to ranking issues in Asia, and has been developed by Kaoru Ishikawa, the pioneer of Japanese Quality. The Fishbone diagram uses graphical means to relate the cause of a problem to the problem itself. It is used when the problem is known, uses brainstorming, and is applicable when there is a communication problem (Ilie & Ciocoiu, 2010). To be effective, the diagram must be constructed by first defining the problem, brainstorming and identifying its causes. In Asia for instance, the policymakers must choose critical issues in ranking decisions that need a permanent fix for quality improvement of the higher education systems and then implement change collaboratively. In applying the Fishbone technique to improve the ranking of very few Asian universities, the possible causes should be analyzed in terms of resources, management, and implementation. Essentially, statistical techniques and ranking results may be used to identify areas that need improvement without neglecting national needs. Critiquing QS ranking methodology using Fishborne explanation means that Asia should focus on the problem of Quality, institutional improvement and policy change rather than chasing numbers.

Therefore, the challenge with ranking scores and statistics is how to use them to improve strategies on resource allocation, student support, staff performance evaluation methods and management improvement (see Vernon, Balas, & Momani, 2018). To avoid this flaw in using ranking scores in making a decision, policymakers may need to verify and find out if the ranking scores are reliable in concluding policy decisions. Assumptions can be made based on the guarantee that ranking evaluation is a fair process. Since QS universities have continually tried to show evidence to justify evaluating universities, rankings scores may be used to determine how Asian universities can be improved, and not necessarily to duplicate Western universities' operations to get a spot on the ranking table. On the other hand, most policies based on ranking scores are likely to be unreliable.

Based on the analysis, universities in the Asian region have issues to consider and need to look beyond improvement based on ranking scores. For instance, the age classification of universities impacts the Shanghai rankings (Safón & Docampo, 2020). If we use the assumption of Shanghai in Asian rankings, many of the highly ranked universities in Asia are likely to be older with a strong capacity for research. Thus, the probability that QS ranking has used the proper method for ranking universities in this region may favor these universities. Asian universities probably have more quality capacity, but the ranking scores and statistics are not revealed. In this scenario, it is essential to describe the nature of universities participating in ranking in Asia and determine whether there are universities on the ranking table that can do better and use different statistical methods and criteria.

Universities that rank well in Asia may be historically old and have spent significant resources on research. Though these universities may be doing well in research, how they align ranking scores to achieve Asia's regional and national development goals is unknown. Similarly, the rankings indicators may also favor universities that have published in international peer-review journals with good citation metrics. However, what does this achievement mean for collective universities in Asia regarding capacity development and regional development for global competitiveness? There is a concern that ranking scores and statistics may not be used well to achieve the growth of other universities because the purpose of ranking is competition, and competitors are reticent to collaborate or share knowledge.

2   Purpose and Methodology of Rankings in Asia

The purpose and methods of ranking are to show participating universities that they are competing on an equal level (see Horstschräer, 2012). This is not true for Asian universities and other institutions in developing countries

(Chou, Lin, & Chiu, 2013). Nevertheless, the objectives and purpose of rankings, including methodology, need specific clarity. Clarity should include the reason for criteria, weighting, decision process, and peer-review process. All these objectives together with ranking purposes may provide more confidence about rankings. The challenge is how to bring this complexity together. The current ranking criteria provide complexity and reason it may be challenging to convince developing countries that the methods used to rank their universities are fair.

The methodologies for ranking universities also provide interesting views about power and politics in global higher education (Stack, 2021). The method elaborates the conscious and unconscious intention of rankers. It also unveils the philosophies of higher education according to the people deciding on the criteria. The conflicts regarding resource sharing among and between universities of different statuses may be motivated by understanding methodologies. In most cases, ranking methods are inadequate and unclear, and ranking activities may not be trusted (Dasdan, Van Lare, & Zivaljevic, 2020). Therefore, the rankings methodology raised several conceptual and thinking issues for rankers, ranking, and ranked. One way to approach this problem is to articulate the technical aspect of rankings in the report to show more clarity and fairness. Many ranking agencies have tried to show this, yet more detail is needed in terms of the design, review process and evaluation used.

Despite suspicion around methodology used for rankings, the rankings result in Asia, particularly in the case of Taiwan, seem to be helping decision-making in their higher education systems (Lo, 2014). Whether the decisions made based on ranking scores are valid or not has to do with national observable performance indicators. For instance, in Asia, we can only assume that the indicators used to measure performance and results were assessed based on a fair instrument or a reliable scale for participating universities, not treating them as homogenous institutions. The issue of reliability needs to be considered seriously for rankers as it provides confidence around rankings results.

As of 2021, the population of Asia was about 4.6 billion people, 5,984 higher education institutions (in 2020), with approximately 12 million students in Southeast Asia. The population and economy in this region provide higher education opportunities to expand continuously. Therefore, measuring the performance of the Quality of higher education provisions is vital. Also, performance statistics should not be misleading, and ranking results are very important in Asia for all these reasons. To decide whether Asian higher education needs ranking for their institutions is a question of purpose. The national quality assurance framework needs reform to become a check and balance for external evaluators or ranking organizations. While this is important, to what extent should rank statistics, methods, and results directly affect Asia's higher education governance affairs?

One important aspect of ranking methods is communicating the ranking report to consumers of rankings. Could there be a situation where the language used to share the results paints the methodology as valid and fair but only in the text? There is an idea that may be communicated by strong narratives or focusing on how consideration of various statistics options was tested to ensure weighting and evaluation of universities equally. The methodology is one key factor to justify fairness, yet it could be used to communicate different things in the report such as power that goes with rankings. This fairness argument can be determined by the consumer of ranking, not the rankers. Often, the critique of hierarchies focuses on technical aspects such as the design of the questionnaire and statistics used for evaluation. It is essential to also consider the methodology used in ranking universities in developing countries. Suppose rankers communicate and persuade participants or users of rankings that the ranking table is reliable for making institutional decisions. In that case, we need to reflect on those decisions. It is unlikely that the report will expressly indicate all implications of ranking results for decision-making. Still, the tone of the message could show that the ranking results are the final verdict to judge the performance of universities in different locations with different characteristics. When Global South academics challenge rankings results, there is a possibility that rankers will be more serious about showing the effect of conscious and unconscious bias in the review process.

Thus, numbers on the ranking table communicate the power of the elites in the society (Palfreyman & Tapper, 2012). Therefore, rankers hold responsibility for showing how their methods and processes ensure social justice. The imperialism ideology in rankings is why rankings' methodology is problematic in the Global South (Lloyd & Ordorika, 2021). Rankings results seem predictable and seem to dominate and change management orientations in the Global South. The power relation is a reason to question how methods are validated and to what extent the decision that went into the procedures is democratic. Imperialization in rankings and methodology is evident throughout the process, from the criteria to be a participating member to nomination or who reviews the performance of universities. This situation also influences international student mobility and it's dynamic in Asia.

The growth of international students and ranking results are moving in the same direction in Asia (Baty, 2010). The methodology should be valid; otherwise, rankings unknowingly may deceptively control students' migration from one region to another. Many Asian students left their country of origin believing the universities' methods, numbers, and positions they see on the rankings table (see Jeremic & Jovanovic-Milenkovic, 2014). Parents also invest well in the cost of international education for their children based on the ranking scores. If the methodology is wrong, scores will not be reliable and, thus, affect internationalization. The race for status, prestige, and recognition will never make the methodology of ranking fair to the Global South. Statistics on international student mobility, especially in Japan, indicate that more Asian students will choose top-ranked universities (Ishikawa, 2009) without any attention to the factors responsible for their rankings. This situation makes the competition for the top 100 best universities fierce and methodologically complicated.

Should national policies have challenged rankings results that proportionate bias and measures quality based on an unclear methodology? We would like to know why a policy of this nature fails or at what stage policy on rankings becomes a problem. The global policy on international higher education or student mobility wants to facilitate integration by recruiting more international students, embracing ranking measures of Quality, and making funding available based on rankings. In practice, what happens to these policies, especially in Asia? Are they taken into account in the analysis of ranking methodology literature? There could also be some systemic problems or issues that may be affecting the shift, change, fluctuations, or noise in the ranking data that rankers provide to users. We can understand this well when rankings allow inclusivity in the decision-making process for methodological validity. So, there is a misalignment in methodology and ranking intention for users.

Should national and regional ranking systems become more important than global ranking due to their uniqueness? This is a conceptual question that requires empirical evidence to judge it. What is perhaps essential to desire is an institutional culture of Quality supported by policies and resources. For instance, several regional organizations evaluate performance and Quality in Asia, while some also promote strategies for integration in qualification recognition, articulation, and quality assurance in higher education. These organizations mostly copy their methods and operation from ranking organizations or similar organizations in the West. In Asia, where resources and capacity building remain limited, regional organizations or associations can appraise the ranking industry of their ability to contribute to their methodology because Asian universities are participating in rankings.

Likewise, a conceptual clarification of what rankings means for power should be reflected in the methodology. The message in rankings is that the evaluation methods are well-considered, and weighting is evaluated on the same scale for all participating universities. The assumption is that all universities are similar and assessed based on that philosophy. Even in the case of Asia, where QS decided to reduce weighting for research, it still cannot justify equality consideration in global university rankings. The big flaw is that the model of rankings and methodology was neither applied nor were stakeholders in the Global South consulted. The model needs to be further critiqued for narrowly omitting and removing this element in evaluating instruments used to measure performance for all universities. We need to understand how these methodological approaches affect rankings globally and in Asia. This justification is difficult but needed; otherwise, it is impossible to prove that ranking is not about the Western elite's ability to control knowledge production in the South. Rankers need to show this through the reports and publications.

Around 5% of the global universities and ranking methodologies provide a stable result for about 1,000 universities (Rauhvargers, 2011). While there is an impression that ranking is part of a vital globalization agency and factors that encourage massive investment in higher education sectors, we also need to talk about data usage. The source of data which forms part of rankings' evaluation was a major concern when ranking was first introduced in 2003. The use of data about students, parents and professors and other people in the institution also formed a major issue in the methodological approach to ranking. Despite the critique and writing on this, much has not changed to show the proper use of data collected for rankings.

Hazelkorn (2017) has emphasized the significance of rankings in Asia and their relation to world-class rhetoric. Therefore, the impact of rankers on ranked institutions or universities that want to be ranked could make data collection and usage problematic, including policy on higher education and public policy (Marginson & Van der Wende, 2007). This is why measuring research measures creates unnecessary competition among universities (see Hazelkorn, 2009). It should be noted that Asian higher education has been put to race with other universities in the West because of the oversimplifying roles and significance of rankings to higher education performance data. This also explains why countries like India consider rankings important (Yeravdekar & Tiwari, 2014). As ranking continues to drive higher education reforms in Europe (see Hazelkorn & Ryan, 2013) and will also do so in Asia. However, these two regions require a different approach to reform, which will also determine the type of data needed to give or collect to inform decisions.

Many of the reforms in higher education consider the internationalization agenda. This is why rankings are now a new name for internationalization, the education market, and globalization because of their role in the world economy (Hazelkorn, 2017). But if ranking is based on convenient data available or supplied by the participating institutions (Harvey, 2008), how much then should the results of these data determine reforms or shape higher education and policies globally? If that is the case, higher education will continue to be controlled and directed by global and local forces (King, 2009). Recently, these forces have been profoundly determined by the activity's rankings, which explains why ranking criteria and methods are for status or reputation (Tilak, 2016). It is also unlikely that the race for status and ranking could have changed the finance and budget pattern of the universities (Douglass, 2016) in the process of striving for status and reputation. This shows a significant shift in geopolitics and geoeconomics in higher education and rankings (Jöns & Hoyler, 2013). Finally, if the rankings sample population of participating institutions in ranking exercises did not cover 90% of the 1500 universities globally (Hazelkorn, 2011), how do we generalize the ranking results to measure higher education's global performance? Among other things, ranking continues to ignore national objectives in its methods (O'Connor, 2021).

3 Concluding Thoughts

It can, therefore, be concluded that ranking indicators have given a particular impression about who controls and influences knowledge creation. It does not clarify assumption that all participating universities are playing on an equal level of resources and capacity. This is the assumption made by the methodology and criteria used for ranking institutions in Asia. Since Asian elite universities rely more on government funding and international collaboration, many expect to collaborate with universities in Western Europe and Northern America when government funding is declined.

Similarly, there have been constant efforts to ensure fairness and transparency in applying ranking criteria across universities of various statuses. However, the revisions of criteria often ignore the fundamental problem of inequality in ranking methodology and standards. Instead, it focuses more on expansion and creating awareness of ranking globally. There are instances where specific metrics and weighting were adopted to rank Asian higher education institutions. Nevertheless, the consideration was based on the level of resources in relation to universities in western Europe and northern America. This metrics reflects how Asian universities perceived in the region compared to other universities globally. Still, determining the impact of this methodology on Asian universities' reputation in terms of global competitiveness remains challenging though they feature among the top-ranked universities in 2022.

As higher education expands globally with more accountability demanded by the various stakeholders, rankings remain one of the crucial options to judge Quality and performance in higher education in Asia. One of the critiques is based on the motivation for ranking Asian universities with a different methodology or criteria. In other words, it seems rankings criteria benefit elite universities, especially those in North America and Western Europe. The universities in these regions have produced more Nobel laurels and have more research output and funding than all the universities in Asia. These circumstances may further prove that the narrative of rankings is embedded in the illusion of globalization and neoliberal philosophy.

Globalization should promote collaboration while facilitating knowledge sharing. This has become difficult as the top universities remain high in the ranking league because they are well-resourced to produce most research. Likewise, many academics in developing countries are few on editorial boards or unable to publish in many high impact academic journals. International publication and strong collaboration are part of the critical criteria for QS and THE rankings, which perpetuate these existing conditions. Consequently, members of the board of major ranking organizations are not often from Asia or other developing countries. In most cases, Asia and other developing countries are not part of policy formulations, reviews, or development that lead to the ranking criteria.

As a result, higher education market, power and politics are also driven by high tuition fees, particularly for international students, to show their high rankings. Using high costs to signal Quality and elite status is unfair because international students are not likely to get into the same programs for lesser tuition fees even in their home countries. Western universities want wealthy international students who can afford their status and fees to improve their economy. Exemplifying this statement is the fact that there are more Asian students in North American elite universities and Europe than in any other country. Evidently, students from this region consider rankings and status a major factor in their application. One major issue is that many of these students remain in developed countries after their studies, which causes brain drain in their home countries and knowledge loss. Another dimension of this issue is that elite universities in the West compete to push forward knowledge produced by them, thus relegating knowledge coming from developing countries. As a result, higher education's purpose has been diluted, which led to cases of unethical practices among elite universities in the quest to be at the top of the ranking table.

Finally, Asian students and universities are constantly structured to resemble or assimilate those in a European or North American system. This is reflected in the recruitment of academics and the constant attempt to promote Western culture and languages. Asian graduates from elite western's universities tend to believe they are civilized and globalized because of the status that their universities carry. Many companies in developing countries prefer graduates from these well-ranked universities, particularly in North America, for employment. This has led to inequality and unfair treatment for graduates who attended local institutions, not on the league table. There is a notion that the graduates from non-ranked universities will not perform well in job market, and attending ranked universities abroad means high quality. Thus, ranking narratives and ideologies are further deepened into global inequality and seem to confuse the national identity of many young graduates in Asia.

References

Al-Bashir, A. (2016). Applying total quality management tools using qfd at higher education institutions in gulf area (Case study: ALHOSN University). *International Journal of Production Management and Engineering*, 4(2), 87–98.

Anowar, F., Helal, M. A., Afroj, S., Sultana, S., Sarker, F., & Mamun, K. A. (2015). A critical review on world university ranking in terms of top four ranking systems. In K. Elleithy & T. Sobh (Eds.), *New trends in networking, computing, e-learning, systems sciences, and engineering* (pp. 559–566). Springer. https://doi.org/10.1007/978-3-319-06764-3_72

Atchuthan, Y., & Elangkumaran, P. (2021). A study on the performance of students in English language at GCE ordinary level examinations using the "Fishbone Diagram": Teaching English in the global village. In *Proceedings of the Rajarata University international symposium on English language teaching page.* SSRN. https://ssrn.com/abstract=3948616

Baty, P. (2010). The world university rankings. *Times Higher Education*, 27.

Chan, S. J. (2012). Enhancing global competitiveness: University ranking movement in Asia. *Evaluation in Higher Education*, 6(1), 15–36.

Chou, C. P., Lin, H. F., & Chiu, Y. J. (2013). The impact of SSCI and SCI on Taiwan's academy: An outcry for fair play. *Asia Pacific Education Review*, 14(1), 23–31.

Dasdan, A., Van Lare, E., & Zivaljevic, B. (2020). *How reliable are university rankings?* arXiv preprint arXiv:2004.09006.

Dobrota, M., Bulajic, M., Bornmann, L., & Jeremic, V. (2016). A new approach to the QS university ranking using the composite I-distance indicator: Uncertainty and sensitivity analyses. *Journal of the Association for Information Science and Technology*, 67(1), 200–211.

Fauzi, M. A., Tan, C. N. L., Daud, M., & Awalludin, M. M. N. (2020). University rankings: A review of methodological flaws. *Issues in Educational Research*.

Hallinger, P. (2010). Using faculty evaluation to improve teaching quality: A longitudinal case study of higher education in Southeast Asia. *Educational Assessment, Evaluation and Accountability*, 22(4), 253–274.

Horstschräer, J. (2012). University rankings in action? The importance of rankings and an excellence competition for university choice of high-ability students. *Economics of Education Review, 31*(6), 1162–1176.

Huang, M. H. (2012). Exploring the h-index at the institutional level: A practical application in world university rankings. *Online Information Review*.

Ishikawa, M. (2009). University rankings, global models, and emerging hegemony: Critical analysis from Japan. *Journal of Studies in International Education, 13*(2), 159–173.

Jeremic, V., & Jovanovic-Milenkovic, M. (2014). Evaluation of Asian university rankings: Position and perspective of leading Indian higher education institutions. *Current Science*, 1647–1653.

Katharaki, M., & Katharakis, G. (2010). A comparative assessment of Greek universities' efficiency using quantitative analysis. *International Journal of Educational Research, 49*(4–5), 115–128.

Lloyd, M., & Ordorika, I. (2021). International university rankings as cultural imperialism: Implications for the Global South. In M. Stack (Ed.), *Global university rankings and the politics of knowledge* (p. 25). University of Toronto Press.

Lo, W. Y. W. (2014). *University rankings: Implications for higher education in Taiwan*. Springer Science & Business Media.

Mahassen, N. (2014). *A quantitative approach to world university rankings*. Center for World University Rankings.

Moed, H. F. (2017). A critical comparative analysis of five world university rankings. *Scientometrics, 110*(2), 967–990.

Ozcan, Y. A. (2005). *Quantitative methods in health care management: techniques and applications*. John Wiley & Sons.

Palfreyman, D., & Tapper, T. (2012). *Structuring mass higher education: The role of elite institutions*. Routledge.

Rodriguez, R. R., Saiz, J. J. A., & Bas, A. O. (2009). Quantitative relationships between key performance indicators for supporting decision-making processes. *Computers in Industry, 60*(2), 104–113.

Safón, V., & Docampo, D. (2020). Analyzing the impact of reputational bias on global university rankings based on objective research performance data: The case of the Shanghai Ranking (ARWU). *Scientometrics, 125*(3), 2199–2227.

Sowter, B. (2008). The Times Higher Education Supplement and Quacquarelli Symonds (THES-QS) World university rankings: New developments in ranking methodology. *Higher Education in Europe, 33*(2–3), 345–347.

Stack, M. (Ed.). (2021). *Global university rankings and the politics of knowledge*. University of Toronto Press.

Tarlow, K. R., Brossart, D. F., McCammon, A. M., Giovanetti, A. J., Belle, M. C., & Philip, J. (2021). Reliable visual analysis of single-case data: A comparison of rating, ranking, and pairwise methods. *Cogent Psychology, 8*(1), 1911076.

Uslu, B. (2020). A path for ranking success: what does the expanded indicator-set of international university rankings suggest? *Higher Education, 80*(5), 949–972.

Vernon, M. M., Balas, E. A., & Momani, S. (2018). Are university rankings useful to improve research? A systematic review. *PloS One, 13*(3), e0193762.

CHAPTER 4

Theorizing 'Comparison' in Ranking Systems

Abstract

Comparing institutions that are so different for ranking purposes is problematic (see Daraio, Iazzolino, Laise, Coniglio, & Di Leo, 2021; Huang, 2011). This chapter theorizes the concept of comparison in ranking from totalitarian and pluralistic perspectives. The argument includes how modernization and the concept of nation-building have accelerated change processes in higher education in Asia. Literature on the sociology of higher education and ranking hegemony needs to be explicit about how Asia is likely to be drifting away from the pressure to become similar to higher education in the West (see Ordorika & Lloyd, 2015; Kim, 2011, 2012; Marginson & Ordorika, 2007). How would modernization recreate a new social order and national building in Asia without manifesting the identity of colonizers? This chapter considers the realities of ranking to make conclusions about the need for comparison, status, and reputation to understand the dynamics of power and politics in the Asian social context.

Keywords

globalization – totalitarianism – pluralistic – modernization – nation-building – colonization – decolonization – Asia

1   Introduction

Historically, Western higher education has shaped the socio-cultural and political landscapes of the world (see Van der Wende, 2003; Siddiqui, 2014; Machingambi, 2014; Montgomery, 2014) including the methodology of rankings. In Asia, colonists mostly Europeans influence education development (Booth, 2007) and university rankings (see Lo, 2011). Asian understanding of knowledge and methods of its transmission in higher education are legacies of colonial religion, culture, and identity (see Valencia Caicedo, 2019). The knowledge production process in Asia is either practising or trying to decolonize the curriculum of the West (Lam, 2009; Hallinger, 2011). One would imagine that the Western epistemologies would create objectivism and positivism, where education outcomes can create dignity and happiness for Asian people (see Metzger & Metzger, 2005; Boaz, 2010). Rankings have rather reinforced the competition for higher education to become powerful and perhaps slowly ignoring cultural identity and development in knowledge production.

On the other hand, the relevance of Western epistemologies and methodologies for the region's development remains a critical question in different contexts (see Wijesinghe & Mura, 2018). The relativism of Western epistemologies can be argued for the Asian context because education objectives should provide a sense of fulfilment for the knowers. Instead, the emphasis has been placed on satisfying the indicators of ranking. This chapter examines theories and argues for understanding the purpose of Asian higher education in the context of ranking power.

2   Ranking and National Identity

Higher education is related to broad personal, social, and national purposes (Chan, 2016; Colby, 2020). In the context of objectivism, higher education outcomes should provide happiness and noticeable development for people who have spent money and time to obtain qualifications. On the other hand, other external forces may change this idea and thus cause issues to national cultural identity in Asia (Le, 2013). Still, education is a major agency that has social and political consequences for rankings.

The pedagogical and epistemological power of the Global South has been put to the test since ranking has been introduced globally and in Asia (Shahjahan, Blanco Ramirez, & Andreotti, 2017; Shahjahan, 2016; Vickers, 2020). As such, teaching and learning are now slowly undermining the classroom due to the quest for rankings (see Hallinger, 2014). There is a constant reminder to reflect global competitiveness in the curriculum because graduates are to look for jobs outside their country of origin. By this, ranking may be promoting the West's economic, political, and cultural identities. However, what is the social, political, and economic implications of training graduates for other countries? Global South countries are referred to as 'underdeveloped', 'developing', and 'emerging' countries because these terms connote weakness and show how they should continue to aspire to be like the West, i.e. developed countries. This state of affairs is not fixed, as the narratives can be changed. This type of change requires challenging the connotation that global ranking is vital for a global knowledge society (Frank & Meyer, 2020). The concern should be to address the issue of discrimination and nation-building in Asia's higher education landscape. Therefore, the purpose of higher education and its outcomes in Asia should reflect the social problems facing each country in this region.

The discourse of university rankings for comparison is the philosophy of capitalism (Hay, 2013; Calderon, 2021). Indeed, the philosophical ideologies of neoliberalism and egalitarianism are embedded in the idea of comparing universities for profit gain (see Olson & Slaughter, 2014). Though some might posit that these intentions are debatable, the purpose of rankers is noticeable through the indicators of ranking and methods used to compare the performance of universities globally. The idea that institutions in different contexts need comparison is profoundly problematic and was constructed based on the capitalist view of world-class universities. This idea attempted to re-construct worldviews that universities are similar traditionally, culturally, linguistically and operated under similar economic conditions. This principle makes the whole ideologies around rankings questionable.

How do we reject the ideologies of capitalism and neoliberalism in rankings without neglecting globalization? University world rankings signal a new world order in higher education systems (see Marginson, 2011). On the one hand, ranking systems and the flow of knowledge across borders are all elements of globalization (see Luke, 2005). On the other hand, only a select few determine how knowledge is produced and evaluated on scaling for comparison purposes. The advent of measuring and comparing the performance of universities is identified as fundamentally premised on the reality that numbers measure Quality. Admittedly, the ideology of counting knowledge to compare performance for universities of various demography is challenging.

Asia, for instance, is different linguistically and culturally (Mackerras, 2003), and these differences inform teaching and learning (Lian & Sussex, 2018). Thus, national identity is challenged in Asia (Chan, 2018) because of comparison brought about by rankings into management and leadership of higher education systems. This situation has challenged many academics whose research works must be compared and evaluated in English (Śliwa & Johansson, 2014). Would the language of publishing have influenced the scholarly productivity of Asian researchers and ultimately affected their ranking if the comparison were made with universities with similar languages? Would a comparison among universities of similar linguistic backgrounds affect a researcher's ability to publish in journals predominantly in the West? This particular situation has given rise to policy change and reforms in Asia (Lee, Liu, & Wu, 2020). The reforms only encourage some private universities to focus on promoting and achieving a top position on the ranking table (see Muñoz-Suárez, Guadalajara, & Osca, 2020). This situation is reason certain institutions in Asia deviate from national interest because they would like to be compared to the elite and world-class universities (see Byun, Jon, & Kim, 2013). The gap between national and global in the philosophical issues around comparison and ranking places the aim of ranking into question.

In this sense, the idea of ranking in Asia can be positioned on the Socratic view of university (see Mast, Glance, & Owens, 2011) to understand the wisdom in comparing significantly different things. In Asia, this framing would encounter other ideas around the purpose of education. Understanding the rationale behind such a comparison may guide our comprehension of whether the ranking process is prescriptive or persuasive towards reordering the national identity of Asia. Despite ranking not being compulsory, the media have created a compelling message since 2003. The universities that are well ranked have used rankings to create different impressions to members of society, including students and parents who need to choose quality. Therefore, it is a game of joining or looking for other means of assuring quality outside the so-called elites and world-class universities.

3   Power and Politics in Rankings

The several contentions on whether to compare global universities are questions of power and politics in knowledge production (Van Dijk, 2011; Young, Corriveau, Nguyen, Cooke, & Hinch, 2016). The narrative of comparing universities can fail if subjected to the test of equality and meaning. The Global South needs to reframe the argument around the politics of ranking on instruments to rank and compare universities globally. What Asian universities may consider also includes how to place the argument on the purpose and meaning of comparing Asian universities at the center of the discussion on identity and culture. As such, universities in this region can focus on knowledge that matters for growth and development without being compared. This is a difficult recommendation for capitalists and neoliberalist leaders because ranking in Asia presents complex history, culture, and identity (Mok, 2016; Foog & Hu, 2013). The historical and cultural complexities present in countries of the Global South are sometimes ignored in the critique of rankings. Notably, the social and cultural realities around ranking need further articulation. Asia needs to become aware of its ethnic diversity, languages, and potential influence of rankings in changing its national identity.

To transform university rankings towards national identity, the willingness of rankers to engage global communities, especially consumers of ranking results, is essential. In relation to the conceptual meaning of comparison, bottom-up deliberation may provide an opportunity for rankers to understand how ranking may be of benefit to stakeholders and to what extent its ideologies can be allowed to influence different societies and contexts. It may be essential to be explicit about how ranking could affect a multicultural society and its development in ranking reports. The rankings indicators that seem prescriptive and redirect the purpose of higher education rather than promote synergy among countries and universities also need attention.

Student mobility is also driven by the wisdom and idea of comparison, where students' identity is now significantly affected by ranking scores (Glass & Cruz, 2022). Technology and digital transformation have made ranking messages shared quickly among the younger generation. They use the message to decide on cultural change and the dominant identity to showcase. These students may have experienced social crises and problems in learning due to their choice or choices that ranking presented to them (Ishikawa, 2009). It is essential to ensure quality improvement of rankings, though many constraints ensure that rankers are put under check. Because the business of comparison seems to be showcasing elitism, very few academics from the Global South may contribute to ideologies in ranking. This critical issue has different dynamics in the discussion of colonization and recolonization.

In Asia, we can try to understand decolonization from a distance and near based on politics and policies of regulatory bodies in higher education. It is seen from near because power and politics may influence local universities to be subjected to a new culture in teaching and learning processes. Based on this idea, there might be a need to find a way to suppress external forces interfering with the power to decide on local universities' domestic affairs. Mainly, decolonization from a ranking perspective could mean using national policies to encourage value systems and building a culture of quality that will make universities globally competitive. However, this largely depends on the resources, history, and political landscape of a country.

There are other factors that could be shaping culture and identity of higher education in Asia. The main factor is digital technology that exposes national culture to comparison to other countries (Bozkurt & Sharma, 2022). Responding to changes caused by technology is profound in Southeast Asia especially (Rab, MacDonald, & Riaz, 2019). For instance, the digital transformation and COVID-19 pandemic have changed how we teach, and students learn. During the COVID-19 pandemic, universities had to lecture online, and technology was significant in that regard. Therefore, decolonizing minds towards safeguarding national values and culture might be challenging due to rapid changes among the younger generation and desire for foreign education due to pandemic. Ranking activities will continue to benefit from these opportunities. Local policies can contribute to the promotion of essential knowledge in Asian culture and identity development by minimizing the importance of comparing institutions, which ranking is promoting in the region.

4 Responding to Social Issues

Rankings compare universities to indicate quality and performance mainly. What this comparison provides to ethnic discrimination and social status is unknown. Higher Education has already been criticized for promoting gaps and inequality in society (Wu, Yan, & Zhang, 2020), and ranking expands this gap (Brown, 2018).

Similarly, the middle class in society are likely to be able to pay tuition fees demanded by ranked universities for their children. Subsequently, a further gap will be created by a situation where only children of rich people can participate in politics and strong economic activities. This category of people or upper-middle-class likely to enjoy the activities of ranking because it could help them keep the pattern of power and their status in the society. This is what governments are expected to challenge and respond to through policies.

Meanwhile, it is hope that governments will be able to understand this dynamic and how it might continue to create generational poverty in various countries. Situation where poor kids usually attend universities that are not ranked or belong to upper-class status needs reform The situation where graduates from elite institutions and low status institutions receive discrimination in the job market needs policy review. If these situation remain unchallenged and solved, rankings may be seen as a globalization movement that could endanger the identity and economic power of the poor countries especially.

Therefore, comparing and using ranking results to determine status and economic benefits is problematic. This debate can stir up negative responses from neoliberalists and elites benefiting from poor ideologies and policies. This situation needs a critical engagement where the oppressed need to challenge the narrative that seems to affect national culture identity in knowledge production instead of promoting it. This type of movement where the oppressed attempt to engage in talks with authorities is not new but often dangerous in countries where the system of government sees it as exposing them to the global community. The interaction of global power with higher education politics in developing countries demonstrates that ranking is unnecessary, particularly in countries already divided by race, ethnicity, religion, and class. It is unknown what ranking might be compared to in those countries where results of social issues are known and may have also affected the quality of education.

What is needed is a system of measuring performance that can redress the inequality created by ignorance and comparison.

However, the dynamic of ranking in Asia has allowed us to understand better comparison theory beyond just the numbers. Ranking has revealed how it is essential not to ignore the citizens affected by the politics and policies of ranking. The epistemological diversity will mean considering systemic issues related to social inequality in response to the pressure of ranking. This situation requires developing opportunities for everyone to succeed regardless of race, gender, religious affiliation, and education. Under these circumstances, the need for comparisons will be limited to the national level, and pressure to apply for comparison from ranking will also be reduced. When there is no need to compare income regardless of the kind of education, higher education will focus on quality that promotes social equality instead of status, which is done at the expense of making others poor.

References

Boaz, D. (2010). *Libertarianism*. Simon and Schuster.

Booth, A. E. (2007). *Colonial legacies: Economic and social development in East and Southeast Asia*. University of Hawai'i Press.

Bozkurt, A., & Sharma, R. C. (2022). Digital transformation and the way we (mis)interpret technology. *Asian Journal of Distance Education*.

Byun, K., Jon, J. E., & Kim, D. (2013). Quest for building world-class universities in South Korea: Outcomes and consequences. *Higher Education, 65*(5), 645–659.

Calderon, A. (2021). The geopolitics of university rankings: Not all regions and university networks stand equal. In E. Hazelkorn & G. Mihut (Eds.), *Research handbook on university rankings*. Edward Elgar Publishing.

Chan, R. Y. (2016). Understanding the purpose of higher education: An analysis of the economic and social benefits for completing a college degree. *Journal of Education Policy, Planning and Administration, 6*(5), 1–40.

Chan, S. J. (2018). Changing landscapes of Asian higher education. *Asian Education and Development Studies*.

Colby, A. (2020). Purpose as a unifying goal for higher education. *Journal of College and Character, 21*(1), 21–29.

Daraio, C., Iazzolino, G., Laise, D., Coniglio, I. M., & Di Leo, S. (2021). Meta-choices in ranking knowledge-based organizations. *Management Decision*.

Foog, M., & Hu, E. E. (2013). *Contact zones in internationalizing Asian universities: Identities, spatialities and global imaginations* [Unpublished thesis]. National University of Singapore.

Frank, D. J., & Meyer, J. W. (2020). The university and the global knowledge society. In D. J. Frank & J. W. Meyer (Eds.), *The university and the global knowledge society*. Princeton University Press.

Glass, C. R., & Cruz, N. I. (2022). Moving towards multipolarity: Shifts in the core-periphery structure of international student mobility and world rankings (2000–2019). *Higher Education*, 1–21.

Hay, S. N. (2013). *Asian ideas of East and West*. Harvard University Press.

Hallinger, P. (2011). Developing a knowledge base for educational leadership and management in East Asia. *School Leadership & Management*, *31*(4), 305–320.

Hallinger, P. (2014). Riding the tiger of world university rankings in East Asia: Where are we heading? *International Journal of Educational Management*, *28*(2), 230–245.

Huang, M. H. (2011). A comparison of three major academic rankings for world universities: From a research evaluation perspective. *Journal of Library & Information Studies*, *9*(1).

Ishikawa, M. (2009). University rankings, global models, and emerging hegemony: Critical analysis from Japan. *Journal of Studies in International Education*, *13*(2), 159–173.

Kim, J. (2011). Aspiration for global cultural capital in the stratified realm of global higher education: Why do Korean students go to US graduate schools? *British Journal of Sociology of Education*, *32*(1), 109–126.

Kim, J. (2012). The birth of academic subalterns: How do foreign students embody the global hegemony of American universities? *Journal of Studies in International Education*, *16*(5), 455–476.

Lam, T. P., & Lam, Y. Y. B. (2009). Medical education reform: The Asian experience. *Academic Medicine*, *84*(9), 1313–1317.

Lee, J., Liu, K., & Wu, Y. (2020). Does the Asian catch-up model of world-class universities work? Revisiting the zero-sum game of global university rankings and government policies. *Educational Research for Policy and Practice*, *19*(3), 319–343.

Le Ha, P. (2013). Issues surrounding English, the internationalization of higher education and national cultural identity in Asia: A focus on Japan. *Critical Studies in Education*, *54*(2), 160–175.

Lian, A., & Sussex, R. (2018). Toward a critical epistemology for learning languages and cultures in twenty-first century Asia. In A. Curtis & R. Sussex (Eds.), *Intercultural communication in Asia: Education, language and values* (pp. 37–54). Springer. https://doi.org/10.1007/978-3-319-69995-0_3

Lo, W. Y. W. (2011). Soft power, university rankings and knowledge production: Distinctions between hegemony and self-determination in higher education. *Comparative Education*, *47*(2), 209–222.

Luke, C. (2005). Capital and knowledge flows: Global higher education markets. *Asia Pacific Journal of Education*, *25*(2), 159–174.

Machingambi, S. (2014). The impact of globalization on higher education: A Marxist critique. *Journal of Sociology and Social Anthropology*, *5*(2), 207–215.

Mackerras, C. (2003). *Ethnicity in Asia*. Routledge.

Marginson, S. (2011). The new world order in higher education: Research rankings, outcomes measures and institutional classifications. In M. Rostan & M. Vaira (Eds.), *Questioning excellence in higher education* (pp. 1–20). Sense.

Marginson, S., & Ordorika, I. (2007). *El central volumen de la fuerza* [*The hegemonic global pattern in the reorganization of elite higher education and research*]. United States Social Sciences Research Council (SSRC).

Mast, N. G., Glance, D. G., & Owens, R. A. (2011). Understanding research performance: The evolution of UWA's research management tool, Socrates. In *AC21 international forum 2010: Competition and cooperation among universities in the age if Internationalization* (pp. 207–225). Shanghai Jiao Tong University Press

Metzger, T. A., & Metzger, T. (2005). *A cloud across the Pacific: Essays on the clash between Chinese and Western political theories today*. Chinese University Press.

Mok, K. H. (2016). *The quest for world-class university status: Implications for sustainable development of Asian universities*. Centre for Global Higher Education working paper series.

Montgomery, C. (2014). Transnational and transcultural positionality in globalized higher education. *Journal of Education for Teaching*, *40*(3), 198–203.

Muñoz-Suárez, M., Guadalajara, N., & Osca, J. M. (2020). A comparative analysis between global university rankings and environmental sustainability of universities. *Sustainability*, *12*(14), 5759.

Olson, J., & Slaughter, S. (2014). Forms of capitalism and creating world-class universities. In A. Maldonado-Maldonado & R. Bassett (Eds.), *The forefront of international higher education* (pp. 267–279). Springer. https://doi.org/10.1007/978-94-007-7085-0_20

Ordorika, I., & Lloyd, M. (2015). International rankings and the contest for university hegemony. *Journal of Education Policy*, *30*(3), 385–405.

Rab, M., MacDonald, S., & Riaz, N. (2019, July 1–3). Digital globalisation of knowledge and the impact on higher education in South Asia. In *EDULEARN19 proceedings 11th international conference on education and new learning technologies* (Palma, Spain). IATED Academy.

Shahjahan, R. A. (2016). International Organizations (IOs), epistemic tools of influence, and the colonial geopolitics of knowledge production in higher education policy. *Journal of Education Policy*, *31*(6), 694–710.

Shahjahan, R. A., Blanco Ramirez, G., & Andreotti, V. D. O. (2017). Attempting to imagine the unimaginable: A decolonial reading of global university rankings. *Comparative Education Review*, *61*(S1), S51–S73.

Siddiqui, K. (2014). Higher education in the era of globalization. *International Journal of Humanities and Social Sciences*, *3*(2), 9–32.

Śliwa, M., & Johansson, M. (2014). How non-native English-speaking staff are evaluated in linguistically diverse organizations: A sociolinguistic perspective. *Journal of International Business Studies, 45*(9), 1133–1151.

Valencia Caicedo, F. (2019). Missionaries in Latin America and Asia: A first global mass education wave. In D. Mitch & G. Cappelli (Eds.), *Globalization and the rise of mass education* (pp. 61–97). Palgrave Macmillan. https://doi.org/10.1007/978-3-030-25417-9_3

Van der Wende, M. C. (2003). Globalization and access to higher education. *Journal of Studies in International Education, 7*(2), 193–206.

Van Dijk, T. A. (2011). Discourse, knowledge, power and politics. *Critical Discourse Studies in Context and Cognition, 43*, 27.

Vickers, E. (2020). Critiquing coloniality, 'epistemic violence' and western hegemony in comparative education – The dangers of ahistoricism and positionality. *Comparative Education, 56*(2), 165–189.

Wijesinghe, S. N. R., & Mura, P. (2018). Situating Asian tourism ontologies, epistemologies and methodologies: From colonialism to neo-colonialism. In P. Mura & C. Khoo-Lattimore (Eds.), *Asian qualitative research in tourism* (pp. 97–115). Springer. https://doi.org/10.1007/978-981-10-7491-2_5

Wu, L., Yan, K., & Zhang, Y. (2020). Higher education expansion and inequality in educational opportunities in China. *Higher Education, 80*(3), 549–570.

Young, N., Corriveau, M., Nguyen, V. M., Cooke, S. J., & Hinch, S. G. (2016). How do potential knowledge users evaluate new claims about a contested resource? Problems of power and politics in knowledge exchange and mobilization. *Journal of Environmental Management, 184*, 380–388.

CHAPTER 5

Aligning Rankings to Cultural and Social Identities

Abstract

This chapter covers essential findings that have emerged from the analysis of QS reputation rankings data. While ranking indicators and scores have been criticized, aligning them to the sociocultural identity of Asian Higher Education may be beneficial for development. The literature indicates the need to show the link between university rankings and national identity in Asia (Yonezawa, 2021). This chapter reflects on the purpose of higher education for Asian sustainable development and discusses the implication of using outcomes of ranking scores to determine reputation. The idea of reputation was reconsidered as an opportunity to negotiate collaboration with institutions that need capacity building, especially in research. The chapter concludes that rankings can drive policy on equity, equality, and sustainable development in Asia.

Keywords

rankings – cultural identity – society – development – Asia

1 Introduction

Countries in Asia face increasing demand to ensure that ranking results respond to cultural and social issues (Ganotice, Tang, Tsui, Villarosa, & Yeung, 2017). Culture and history are strongly intertwined with the Asian identity. Thereupon, these factors determine the structure of universities and their governance. The earliest Higher Education rankings were developed in the 1900s in the United States to rearrange society (Geiger, 2017; College Rank, 2021). Thus, the early rankings were exclusively outcome-based (Marginson, 2014) and were helpful in Asian quality indicators (Borsoto, Lescano, Maquimot, Santorce, Simbulan, & Pagcaliwagan, 2014). In 1904, Havelock Ellis studied nurture vs nature and compiled and ranked universities depending on the geniuses that attended them (Myers & Robe, 2009). Consequently, reputational rankings became famous as the significance of institutional reputation substituted student prominence (see Alter & Reback, 2014). Since then, reputational

Higher Education rankings have been a principal approach to creating academic quality rankings.

Higher Education in Southeast Asia remains a state extension regardless of Western modernization influences (Omidifar, Ghaleei, Hasani, & Mousavi, 2018, p. 627). It uses knowledge production to contribute to the public welfare. International issues like health, food security, conflict resolution, and clean water are potential contributions that knowledge produced by Higher Education can make toward general welfare (Tran, Nghia, Nguyen, & Ngo, 2020, p. 281). In Asia, this approach remains distinct compared to other developing countries or Western capitalist nations (Nguyen & Tran, 2018, p. 28). Notwithstanding, Asian countries have considered the need for active engagement in adapting and adopting Western Higher Education practices through ranking systems. While rankings have influenced governance in Asia, it is vital to understand how rankings may have expanded the inequalities and whether it aligns with national cultural identity.

2 Results of Ranking in Asian Higher Education

Recently, three major universities in China have announced their withdrawal from participating in global university rankings to concentrate on locally relevant quality goals (Sharma, 2022). The decision speaks to the purpose and relevance of global rankings to local development. Aside from the relevancy issue, the indicators used to rank Asian Higher Education have been challenged. Yet, universities in Asia, particularly North-East Asian universities, continue to impact global rankings. This impact shows the counterfactual effects of rankings indicators. However, there could be other reasons behind some Asian universities' exemplary performance in the global rankings competition. One is that indicators used to rank Asian universities may have consequence for global ranking indicators. If that were the case, the decision of three Chinese universities to withdraw from global rankings might be justified. Still, this withdrawal may not be forthcoming for many institutions in Southeast Asia since the number of South Asian institutions and those in ASEAN countries represented on the global rankings table are improving. If global rankings outcomes fail to align with cultural characteristics, it might be challenging to determine its purpose in a different context. This situation also signals the need to reflect on other Quality indicators that may have given an advantage to North-East Asian universities, allowing them to dominate Asian rankings over the years.

In 2018, the British Council funded a study on the policies of Higher Education internationalization in ASEAN nations like Cambodia, Brunei, Indonesia,

Malaysia, Laos, Myanmar, Philippines, Vietnam, Singapore, and Thailand (Atherton et al., 2019). The study established the influential role of Higher Education in global relations, hence supporting an aligned and integrated ASEAN community and diplomacy. In such a vibrant and rapidly developing region with over 620 million people, the study found that ASEAN countries emphasize Higher Education mobility and openness at different levels, in accordance with the developmental stage of individual nations (Sier, 2021, p. 16). Despite the investment in internationalization at the regional level, most highly ranked universities remain outside Southeast Asia or ASEAN. The QS ranking measures academic reputation in ASEAN countries using global surveys by asking academics to categorize institutions with the best work within individual expertise fields. It measures the employer reputation indicator based on global surveys, asking the institutional staff to rank universities based on the perception of producing the finest graduates (Quacquarelli Symonds (QS), 2021).

Asian countries need to consider the inconsistency in criteria and indicators of rankings (Huang, 2012). If social inequality were to be addressed by focusing on indicators making universities address poverty (Singh & Khaira, 2018), Asian universities might become agents of actual development. Moreover, focusing on indicators of local relevance might provide institutions with the opportunity to address global problems as well. This approach to understanding Quality indicators and measurement may suggest new trends to end the overreliance on the Western performance metric for global Higher Education. Ending this overdependence involves challenging the West's control and power over universities in emerging and developing countries (Hertig, 2016). This thinking points to ensuring that indicators of global rankings can adapt to national development goals.

Country-specific policies promoting the use of unique indicators different from the commonly known Quality indicators have always been a source of complex and deeply political conflicts in Asia. For instance, the global universities rankings have developed a strong brand, and Chinese universities' decision to stop participation may create tension. Such a decision may affect political and economic relations among countries that supply outputs of Higher Education. If the trend of non-participating in global universities rankings continue, this could also affect student mobility and other academic exchange with Western universities. The consequences stemming from some Asian universities' withdrawal depend on the West's stance on losing control over universities in developing countries. In many Western universities, the financial support for international students and academic mobility is tied to meeting the requirements of criteria and indicators of rankings. The tension that three Chinese universities are creating in the global rankings market by withdrawing signals global Higher Education reform. As a result, it may redefine student and academic mobility patterns and is likely to change the narrative that Western knowledge is the only parameter for determining the Quality indicators to measure global Higher Education performance. In other words, emerging and developing countries may begin to restructure the future of their Higher Education based on the philosophies of the Chinese universities that have stopped participating in rankings. The long-term implication of such a change requires some exploration.

Government regulatory bodies often measure universities' performance based on political indicators of development or agenda. However, this idea may affect efforts to make Asian universities contribute to development. The crux is finding the commonality among these indicators and criteria to ensure that political agendas will not interfere with their effectiveness. Focusing on rankings indicators has put pressure on universities' management and leadership for decades and affects the innovation and effectiveness of government policies. In Asia, it has indirectly changed the universities' focus and mission to serve the purpose of Western economies and development. Locally, it affects workloads, teaching, and learning activities because ranking indicators created a new order in global Higher Education management. Finding synergies among indicators requiring different performance evidence entails carefully considering the meaning of education outcomes for ordinary people in Asia. One way to approach it is to define the purpose of being measured and what the performance means for national development and cultural identity. This action plan may be the beginning of an effective synergy between several indicators to promote cultural identity. For instance, one of the important agendas for ASEAN is to determine steps to ensure that ranking indicators promote the language, culture, and cultural values of member countries. Thus, if ranking outcomes are different, it cannot be used to understand development at a macro level.

Asia and Asian universities are different linguistically, socially, and economically. This understanding should guide government policies for higher education and quality assurance. This acknowledgment aims not to achieve identical culture or common values system but to transform Higher Education towards national development. The aim is to refrain from seeing Asian Higher Education as homogeneous entities and recognize that regional or global policies can influence its identity. Global rankings are responsible for the confusion created in maintaining the identity of national universities. At the regional level, well-ranked universities in Asia may have obtained the Western identity of world-class universities and may participate in policy deliberation differently. Be that as it may, this westernization promotes an elitist status and a 'world-class' culture, encouraging ranked Asian universities to not collaborate with other universities that are not in this circle. This state of affairs is due to rankings motivating elitist universities' change of identity and the difficulty of contributing to local development even though these universities are in Asia. Several regional organizations and quality assurance agencies are eager to promote an identical Asian Higher Education in terms of the quality of qualification through accreditation. This approach is complex. However, it is possible to allow individual countries to use performance indicators to develop their higher education system and determine what higher education outcomes mean for citizens.

The involvement of Western philosophies in performance indicators used to measure global Higher Education suggests several policy reviews for Asia. First, the notion that 'elite' and 'world-class' status needs to be promoted must be reviewed for Asia's cultural protection. Secondly, the peer-review methods giving an unfair advantage to elite universities because of their network also need to be reviewed regarding the impact of this favoritism on the regional development of Asian higher education. The teaching criterion is greatly ignored as a ranking indicator, and this omission in ranking criteria should also be reconsidered for Asia. Also, the relevance of the top 100 Asian universities in global rankings for their culture and history should be determined. These reflections play an essential role in deliberating what is significant for national development regarding higher education performance indicators.

In Asia and elsewhere, education outcomes are often defined by whether graduates can get a job in a relevant field and how employers perceive their skills or qualifications. higher education produced skills are perceptive and primarily determined by the curriculum offered. Global rankings also play an important role in the development of skills. Ranking evaluates universities that have a reputation with employers. While this indicator is economic-based, it also shows that the skills produced by universities are quality indicators based on Western ideologies. Quality should also be defined based on graduates' ability to contribute meaningfully to national development culturally and socially, though this aspect is not measured in global university rankings indicators. For instance, the number of violence, rape cases, suicide incidents, and discrimination that have led to social issues requires graduates equipped to offer solutions, not graduates who can perform only at jobs. Furthermore, national cultural value indicators are based on whether graduates can behave responsibly in society and contribute to world peace. These are the kind of quality indicators that higher education should be promoting, and rankings should also find a way to incorporate them into their evaluation.

3   Evaluating Social Importance in Asia

Asian countries, like many other countries, are facing social issues related to land space, pollution, climate change, violence, immigration issues, ethnic crisis, rapid urbanization, gender revolution, political issues, governance issues, and global warming. Evidently, these forces affect public and higher education policies, as they should inform education outcomes. Concerning the immigration issue, international students have reported visa issues as a hindrance to studying in most Asian countries. The number of international students coming to Asia can improve foreign direct investment in the region and the opportunity to upgrade campus facilities which ultimately could influence ranking scores and development. The importance of this aspect lies in the growth that it can generate in the face of technology and globalization. However, due to the inability to consider the impact of immigration law on international students, Asian countries' development, particularly in Southeast Asia, has been dramatically impacted. As such, rankings and ranking indicators should align with and reflect relevant Asian realities concerning the issues which prevail in the region.

Several Asian countries face social and environmental issues such as environmental pollution. As the Asian population increases, there is also an increase in industrial companies emitting gases harmful to the population's health. Environmental pollution is a global issue and needs particular attention in many Asian countries. The onus falls on Higher Education to produce more skilled and passionate scientists able to offer solutions to climate change and pollution. The production of experts requires a curriculum that understands the dynamics of this problem in Asia. Noticeably, many great Asian scientists migrate to North America and Western Europe. Likewise, international students often choose to remain in their host country after completing their studies abroad, which reduces the expert pool needed to solve environmental issues in their home country. First, ranking narratives motivate students to attain a Western education, mainly when the value systems required from their countries to be considered in ranking leagues are not taught. Resultantly, the move from East to West leads to brain gain for Western countries. Besides the brain drain incurred by Asia, eastern migration to the West depicts the part played by rankings narratives and outcomes in the redirection of skills away from the Global South to the North in the name of world-class university rankings advocacy. Meanwhile, government policies should have made economic and political systems conducive to attracting Asian students back home. The more significant challenge is whether scientists exposed to a new culture and different world-class universities can fit Asia's unique economic and political realities.

Asia is one of the poorest continents in the world, with more than 800 million people still living under less than $1.25 a day and 1.7 billion surviving on less than $2 a day (Kuroda, 2013). Evidently, the issue of poverty affects the continent's security and stability. There have been violence cases in different Asian countries at different levels, particularly in Southeast Asia, where poverty levels are high. The government could hope that Higher Education will assist in producing graduates with entrepreneurial skills to contribute to the continent's development in terms of job creation and investments in sectors such as agriculture to curb the food supply problem.

Ranking indicators or performance quality focus on the peer-review evaluation of research, employability, internationalization, and teaching and learning. The focus of this indicator is to highlight universities with higher scores as a measure of Quality, which has no link to solving poverty and the food supply problem in Asia. In most cases, indicators have changed the curriculum's focus to that of Western elite universities, where existing social issues are different and not the focal point. It is, therefore, incumbent on Higher Education to ensure that research and teaching and learning focus aligns with the social issues of the societies where they operate.

If the gender, wealth, and access to quality education inequality gaps are closed, these issues can be adequately addressed. However, ranking cannot determine whether research outputs address inequality. Rankings could also give more importance to research related to social issues like gender, education opportunities for women, and the creation of wealth through research that provides recommendations for climate change and food supply policies. In other words, indicators should look beyond the number of outputs (quantity) and consider the quality and ability of these outputs to contribute to social development, which is crucial in an Asian context. In developing Asia, 1.7 billion people (45% of the population) lack access to sanitation, and 680 million do not have access to electricity (Kuroda, 2013). Considering that inequality and social problems continue to increase despite an increase in the number of ranked Asian universities, it can be concluded that ranking results are meaningless to Asia's developmental issues.

Though globalization and advanced technology may have advanced knowledge globally, it has also created a deep social gap in Asia. The dynamics of university rankings and their impact on the Higher Education market are troubling. Ranking's influence is felt in the increase of Higher Education costs, making the most attractive programs only accessible to wealthy students who ultimately control the economy after graduation. Ranking is also responsible for graduates who wish to thrive in countries other than their own due to the curriculum promoted by ranking indicators. Asia is considered grounds for cheap labor, into which foreign companies tap to develop their products or make provisions for labor to be exported to other countries. The Philippines is an example of a country where many students aim to look for jobs outside the country before they graduate. Yet, Asian qualifications are not considered equal to Western counterparts, except for qualifications attained from ranked universities or institutions that comply with ranking indicators.

The ranking's reputation indicator presents elite universities with the opportunity to exercise power over the powerless or exploit their labor forces. Therefore, the QS six indicators might promote the elite's power and the ability to use this to achieve their development. There should be efforts in Asia to make the culture of Higher Education respond to developmental needs. To remain locally relevant and be responsive concerning regional issues, education goals should reflect continental problems needing solving.

Higher education's internationalization through rankings is expected to benefit faculty, students, and research to address inequalities. Higher education Institutions are responsible agencies for practicing that can promote global peace awareness through activities aiming at uplifting individual aspiration and growth. Global peace can only be achieved if beneficiaries of Higher Education outputs are considered in designing performance indicators for higher education. There are systemic and structural inequalities in Asia, and solutions require some adjustment in the conditions and frameworks that define higher education purpose.

The trend of competitions created by rankings is expected to take another dimension in the future. The institution strategies to cope with the new trends set by Chinese universities will vary and depend on institutions' status in the global Higher Education space. For small institutions, rankings indicators may be used to measure their performance or to drive change in their institutions. However, it becomes complex when more and more institutions consider alternate methods to measure their institutions' performance. On the other hand, higher education's global competitiveness may now be determined from the global South and not necessarily from the usual weighting and metrics known to institutions. Collaborated efforts have been made in the Global South and among Asian countries to offer their Higher Education Institutions the much-needed opportunity to access and permit more scientific productions based on Southern epistemologies and theories.

The revolution taking place in rankings will affect research and cross-border education or knowledge transfer. However, this course of action was only a means to an end, ensuring that consumers of rankings derive sustainable benefits from their historical and cultural identity. Meanwhile, the growth of rankings in the Asian region can be monitored and evaluated based on responses to changes, reforms, and the revolution that is rapidly changing the Higher Education landscape globally.

4 Concluding Thoughts

Higher Education has been significantly challenged by the forces of capitalism, colonialism, elitism, racism, and others, which remain a significant reason for introducing ranking. Rankings' aim may not be to promote negativity or hinder the development of the Asian region, but analyses show it may have inadvertently influenced it. National cultural identity cannot be undermined in providing quality Higher Education. Similarly, social issues cannot be ignored for ranking to be accepted in developing countries.

Though nationalism is not promoted, Asian countries need to rethink the purpose of ranking and its role in achieving sustainable development. Collaborations and regional partnerships are growing in different regions of Asia to ensure education addresses relevant developmental issues. Moreover, it is essential to see regional associations contribute toward Higher Education policies by building on Asian history and different cultural values.

Regarding student mobility, rankings supply students worldwide at the expense of Asia since the region has been unable to attract international students from the West. Furthermore, ranking assisted universities in the Global North in attracting wealthy students from Asia. Consequently, there is a pressing need for Asian regional organizations to remedy this state of affairs by determining the best use of Higher Education resources.

Regarding research publication, Asia could identify an aspect of publication that promotes the uniqueness of individual countries on the continent. It would be judicious for quality research journals to focus on matters from social issues faced by Asian countries to general knowledge and findings that will lead to the continent's economic, social, and political development.

Therefore, Higher Education in Asia should emphasize the promotion of national values rather than adhering to ranking systems that indirectly influence learning culture. Asian societies need a framework that could encourage equality, civil rights, and solutions to issues causing poverty. Resolving social issues will increase purchasing power and the ability to afford school fees. An economic turnaround will limit illiteracy, particularly among young women vulnerable to sexual molestation and forced labor in some parts of central Asia. Education should promote dignity and enforce the cultural value of respect for individuals, not necessarily be structured by ranking systems. When Asian society and education promote good values, common problems such as health, sanitation, and security, will be addressed and solutions offered. Evidently, good values are difficult to quantify or evaluate in rankings reviews since it does not promote the neoliberal agenda.

Hence, the Western monopoly on knowledge and knowledge application is allowed due to policy ignorance in many developing countries. The knowledge quantified to show the superiority of elite universities or individuals is anti-social and downplays important values in socio-economic and political development. Western capitalism manifests through the ranking model and knowledge globalization.

The global ranking system of comparing institutions requires assessment and evaluation where stakeholders will determine whether this system has financial, cultural, institutional, and national ramifications. Such reviews should provide the opportunity to organize conferences and forums to discuss the value of ranking, including other issues related to capitalism and globalization's influence on the affairs of Asia.

Importantly, competition due to ranking and comparing global Higher Education performance needs to be significantly reduced. Corruption and the manipulation of systems that perpetuate poverty and inequality in many Asian countries can be attributed to competition. Thus, reforms in the governance of Higher Education that regain power from the global market and prevent institutions from being managed by students or managers rather than intellectuals are required. This step in Higher Education reform is crucial as managers consider students to be customers and staff members' primary mandate to satisfy the university's customers. On the one hand, intellectuals are key role players in the governance of institutions. They will endeavor to build a culture of academic excellence and ensure education outcomes that impact society. On the other hand, managers pursue ranking results at the expense of status and place too much focus on the institutional image to be compared with capitalist/colonial institutions.

Likewise, international treaties on academic mobility from South to North need to be reanalyzed to determine whether they contribute to the national development. Many researchers from the West have used international academic mobility as an opportunity to develop their countries. They have made the mobility program attractive using funding that attracts brilliant scientists from Asian countries. Moreover, internationalization is still relevant, but its motivation and aims should be revised to ensure that it does not offer an unfair advantage to certain countries at the expense of others. Ranking has made international mobility attractive to Asian students and has also used ranking power to make talent suppliers eager to export their best for funding promises. This can be renegotiated, but it should start with downplaying the ranking scores' narrative and influence.

With the revolution starting in Asia, it will likely reach other developing countries that feel the need to decolonize knowledge and their citizens' minds to facilitate national development. Indeed, the decolonization of research, curriculum, and other aspects of education is unavoidable. The value of national innovation needs to be incorporated into the curriculum, and ample opportunity to practice professions should be provided before and after graduation. Essentially, challenging Western knowledge dominance requires leaders in developing countries to showcase a good value system in their governance. However, developing countries often lack the ability to be role models of what is exemplary, while the lack of growth opportunities hinders any breakthrough or development. If this problem is addressed, Western education could be removed from its pedestal, and development will be feasible in technology innovation, digital transformation, and job security. Decolonizing the ranking knowledge and narrative requires more effort from the leaders at all levels.

References

Douglass, J. A. (2016). How rankings came to determine world class. In J. A. Douglass (Ed.), *The new flagship university: International and development education* (pp. 9–29). Palgrave Macmillan. https://doi.org/10.1057/9781137500496_1

Ganotice Jr., F. A., Tang, H. H. H., Tsui, G., Villarosa, J. B., & Yeung, S. S. (2017). Globalization of world university rankings and its impact on Asian universities. In K. Downing & F. A. Ganotice Jr. (Eds.), *World university rankings and the future of higher education* (pp. 329–344). IGI Global.

Hertig, H. P. (2016). *Universities, rankings and the dynamics of global higher education: Perspectives from Asia, Europe and North America.* Springer.

Huang, M. H. (2012). Opening the black box of QS world university rankings. *Research Evaluation, 21*(1), 71–78.

Kuroda, H. (2013). *Asia's challenges.* Retrieved May 1, 2020, from https://www.oecd.org/economy/asia-challenges.htm

Lee, J., Liu, K., & Wu, Y. (2020). Does the Asian catch-up model of world-class universities work? Revisiting the zero-sum game of global university rankings and government policies. *Educational Research for Policy and Practice, 19*(3), 319–343.

Marginson, S. (2010). Higher Education in the global knowledge economy. *Procedia Social and Behavioral Sciences, 2*(5), 6962–6980.

Sharma, Y. (2022). Three major universities quit international rankings. *World Universities News.* Retrieved May 15, 2022, from https://www.universityworldnews.com/post.php?story=20220511170923665#:~:text=The%20three%20prestigious%20universities%2C%20Renmin,autonomy%E2%80%9D%20and%20%E2%80%9Ceducation%20with%20Chinese

Singh, G., & Khaira, K. S. (2018). Governance and poverty reduction in the South Asian countries: A perspective from management education. *SAMVAD*, *16*(2), 53–62.

Yonezawa, A. (2021). Reimaging university identities through rankings in Japan: The transformation of national policies and university behaviours in the broader East Asian context. In E. Hazelkorn & G. Mihut (Eds.), *Research handbook on university rankings*. Edward Elgar Publishing.

APPENDIX

Overall Score and Ranking Dataset

Year	Code	Institution name	Country	Size	Focus	Research	Age	Status	Score	Academic reputation rank	Academic reputation score
2020	1			2	2	1	4	2	34	249	60.7
2020	2			1	3	2	5	1	24.6	341	52.9
2020	3			0	3	1	2	1	18.3	456	35.1
2020	4			1	1	2	4	2	4.7	501+	15
2020	5	Bandung Institute of Technology (ITB)	Indonesia	2	2	2	4	2	39.3	209	39.8
2020	6	Beihang University	China	2	2	2	4	2	15.5	501+	6
2020	7	Beijing Normal University	China	2	2	2	5	2	39	211	12.3
2020	9	Ben Gurion University of the Negev	Israel	2	3	2	4	2	16.4	499	19.1
2020	10	Chang Gung University	Taiwan	1	1	2	3	1	3.8	501+	4.5
2020	11	Chiba University	Japan	2	3	2	5	2	14.6	501+	4.9
2020	12	Chulalongkorn University	Thailand	3	3	1	5	2	62.4	108	56.5
2020	13	Chung-Ang University	South Korea	2	3	1	5	1	14.1	501+	21.1
2020	14	City University of Hong Kong	Hong Kong	1	2	2	3	2	59	122	41.3
2020	15	Dongguk University	South Korea	2	3	1	5	1	10.4	501+	7
2020	17	Ewha Womans University	South Korea	2	3	1	5	1	22.4	371	16.5
2020	18	Fudan University	China	3	3	2	5	2	83.4	60	93.8
2020	19	Gwangju Institute of Science and Technology (GIST)	South Korea	0	1	2	3	2	11	501+	3.9
2020	20	Hanyang University	South Korea	2	3	2	4	1	46.8	169	68.4
2020	21	Harbin Institute of Technology	China	3	1	2	4	2	21.8	383	7.3

Employer reputation rank	Faculty student score	Faculty student rank	Citations per faculty score	Citations per faculty rank	International faculty score	International faculty rank	International students score	International students rank	Overall score
124	98.6	41	1.2	601+	40.8	390	26.1	471	**43.1**
154	63.1	228	15.2	601+	90.2	166	64.6	212	**38.7**
272	30.2	504	13.4	601+	100	8	100	5	**29.6**
501+	7.4	601+	94.9	22	7	601	2.6	601	**24.4**
236	51.3	296	3.7	601+	29.2	465	1.6	601	**32.3**
501+	31.8	477	55.8	174	10.1	601	6.2	601	**25.2**
501+	31.2	485	48.6	245	23.6	514	31.4	416	**35.7**
483	18.2	601+	53.3	195	70.1	250	21.3	511	**27.4**
501+	59.3	245	50.2	227	3.7	601	8.1	601	**24.5**
501+	79.8	145	14.7	601+	8.5	601	6.1	601	**26**
141	25.6	573	8.5	601+	11.5	601	2.5	601	**38.3**
436	77.3	157	11	601+	16.5	595	29.6	433	**27.8**
230	89.7	81	89.4	34	100	14	95.3	80	**73.6**
501+	82	134	9.1	601+	14.4	601	35.1	385	**25.6**
501+	82.7	129	13.3	601+	10.5	601	36.9	371	**32.3**
34	86.5	99	57.8	157	92.7	147	42.9	329	**78.6**
501+	36.8	425	100	5	10.1	601+	7.2	601	**33.1**
103	77.2	161	30.8	431	25.4	496	34.8	390	**50.3**
501+	52.6	286	72.9	80	10.8	601	10	601	**35.7**

Year	Code	Institution name	Country	Size	Focus	Research	Age	Status	Score	Academic reputation rank	Academic reputation score
2020	23			2	3	2	5	2	39.4	206	38.5
2020	24	Hiroshima University	Japan	2	3	2	4	2	24.1	348	9.7
2020	25	Hitotsubashi University	Japan	1	0	1	5	2	21.2	388	66.8
2020	26	Hokkaido University	Japan	2	3	2	5	2	56.3	131	47.1
2020	27	Hong Kong Baptist University (HKBU)	Hong Kong	1	3	2	3	2	18.6	446	15.4
2020	28	Huazhong University of Science and Technology	China	3	3	2	4	2	19.2	434	23.4
2020	29	HUFS – Hankuk (Korea) University of Foreign Studies	South Korea	2	2	1	4	1	12.2	501+	20.1
2020	30	Indian Institute of Science (IISc) Bangalore	India	0	0	2	5	2	33.3	254	16.2
2020	31	Indian Institute of Technology Bombay (IITB)	India	1	2	2	4	2	54.5	138	71.2
2020	32	Indian Institute of Technology Delhi (IITD)	India	1	2	2	4	2	46.8	168	63
2020	33	Indian Institute of Technology Guwahati (IITG)	India	1	2	2	3	2	11.7	501+	15.2
2020	34	Indian Institute of Technology Kanpur (IITK)	India	1	2	2	4	2	29.9	284	32.4
2020	35	Indian Institute of Technology Kharagpur (IITKGP)	India	1	1	2	4	2	26.6	317	41.1
2020	36	Indian Institute of Technology Madras (IITM)	India	1	2	2	4	2	35.3	236	47.3
2020	37	Indian Institute of Technology Roorkee (IITR)	India	1	1	2	5	2	13.7	501+	19.6

APPENDIX

Employer reputation rank	Faculty student score	Faculty student rank	Citations per faculty score	Citations per faculty rank	International faculty score	International faculty rank	International students score	International students rank	Overall score
247	77.9	153	43.4	295	71.1	247	11.6	601	48.2
501+	84.1	122	15.4	601+	13.8	601	17.1	567	32.2
106	35.9	433	4.3	601+	29.2	466	21.5	510	25.8
187	84.4	119	34.2	391	20	548	15	592	52.9
501+	41.5	371	49.8	230	99.9	61	90.4	109	36.9
397	17.3	601+	68.1	100	12.7	601	6.6	601	28.2
455	82.7	128	2.2	601+	40.3	394	40.9	341	28
501+	53.2	280	100	2	1.5	601	1.8	601	45.9
95	45.8	326	54.6	184	3.4	601	1.6	601	49.4
118	23.3	601+	80.6	52	3.3	601	1.5	601	46.2
501+	18.7	601+	71.2	89			1.5	601	24.3
297	14.1	601+	82.3	49	1.9	601	1.3	601	34.8
231	21.6	601+	78.4	62	5.3	601	1	601	35.2
183	28	540	56.4	168	3.4	601	1.6	601+	36.1
467	11.7	601+	93.8	25			3	601	28.8

Year	Code	Institution name	Country	Size	Focus	Research	Age	Status	Score	Academic reputation rank	Academic reputation score
2020	38	Jilin University	China	3	3	2	4	2	16.6	494	12.6
2020	39	KAIST – Korea Advanced Institute of Science and Technology	South Korea	1	2	2	3	2	85	58	74.5
2020	40	Keio University	Japan	3	3	2	5	1	51.4	149	77.2
2020	41			0	0	2	2	2	9.3	501+	9.7
2020	42			3	3	2	4	2	28.5	298	36.8
2020	43			1	2	2	4	2	26.8	315	20.1
2020	44			3	3	2	4	2	28.3	301	16.8
2020	45	Kobe University	Japan	2	3	2	4	2	24.6	340	27.4
2020	46			1	2	2	3	1	16.3	501+	31.4
2020	47	Korea University	South Korea	2	3	2	5	1	70	86	85
2020	48	Kyoto University	Japan	2	3	2	5	2	98.7	20	92.5
2020	49	Kyung Hee University	South Korea	2	3	2	4	1	27.1	310	32.4
2020	50	Kyushu University	Japan	2	3	2	5	2	55.5	133	49.2
2020	51			2	1	1	2	2	12.9	501+	14.8
2020	52			2	2	0	4	2	7	501+	6.1
2020	53	Mahidol University	Thailand	2	3	2	4	2	38.9	212	33.2
2020	54	Nagoya University	Japan	2	3	2	5	2	60.5	118	38.6
2020	55	Nanjing University	China	3	3	2	5	2	60.7	117	30.3
2020	56	Nankai University	China	2	3	2	5	2	22.3	375	5.4
2020	57	Nanyang Technological University (NTU)	Singapore	2	3	2	3	2	92.1	37	93.8
2020	58	National Central University	Taiwan	1	2	2	4	2	23	361	19.5
2020	59	National Cheng Kung University	Taiwan	2	3	2	4	2	40.8	196	53.4

APPENDIX

Employer reputation rank	Faculty student score	Faculty student rank	Citations per faculty score	Citations per faculty rank	International faculty score	International faculty rank	International students score	International students rank	Overall score
501+	53.1	281	25.2	482	13.9	601	3	601	24.5
88	73.9	175	98.1	16	25.8	494	10.1	601	77.9
84	62.2	233	9.4	601+	13.2	601	11.3	601	44
501+	77.3	158	42.2	307	100	9	55.6	264	36.5
260	71.3	190	38.6	339	99	80	60.6	234	45.2
457	85.2	111	40.1	327	100	20	21.8	506	44
501+	69	198	15.9	601+	91.5	157	11.3	601	35.2
342	58.3	251	15.4	601+	10.2	601	9	601	28.4
304	49.8	305	18.4	580	39.9	398	6.7	601	25.7
59	83.1	126	35.4	381	15.2	601	44.7	317	63.4
41	96.3	56	53.2	196	15.4	601+	17.5	564	80.5
298	87.8	94	18.4	578	15.2	601	41.1	338	38.3
172	85.6	106	32.6	411	18.6	565	21.5	509	52.9
501+	93	70	1.4	601+	32.3	442	6.1	601	27.5
501+	94.1	64	1	601+	17.1	584	17.7	557	24.3
289	61.4	236	6.7	601+	8.9	601	5.9	601	33.4
246	90.6	79	37.3	361	17.7	578	21.3	513	55.8
318	31	487	84.2	47	68.6	258	11.1	601	54.5
501+	28.4	532	63.2	127	30.9	452	8	601+	29.8
35	93.9	66	88.8	36	100	21	74.2	169	91.8
469	32.8	462	36.3	374	20.7	541	20.3	528	27.1
152	42.5	360	39.7	329	17.7	579	26.4	466	40.4

Year	Code	Institution name	Country	Size	Focus	Research	Age	Status	Score	Academic reputation rank	Academic reputation score
2020	60	National Chiao Tung University	Taiwan	1	2	2	5	2	28.9	293	52.1
2020	61	National Taiwan Normal University	Taiwan	1	2	2	4	2	28.8	296	11.4
2020	62	National Taiwan University (NTU)	Taiwan	3	3	2	4	2	89.8	41	82.4
2020	63	National Taiwan University of Science and Technology	Taiwan	1	1	2	3	2	24.4	346	30.6
2020	64			2	1	2	5	2	18.7	444	45
2020	65	National Tsing Hua University	Taiwan	2	2	2	4	2	47.5	165	59.6
2020	66	National University of Sciences and Technology (NUST) Islamabad	Pakistan	1	2	2	3	2	16.4	501+	39.4
2020	67	National University of Singapore (NUS)	Singapore	3	3	2	5	2	99.8	11	99.2
2020	68	National Yang Ming University	Taiwan	0	3	2	3	2	14.4	501+	16.9
2020	69	Osaka University	Japan	2	3	2	4	2	80.8	62	67.5
2020	70	Pakistan Institute of Engineering and Applied Sciences (PIEAS)	Pakistan	0	1	2	2	2	5.4	501+	4.6
2020	71	Peking University	China	3	3	2	5	2	99.1	16	99.6
2020	72	Pohang University of Science and Technology (POSTECH)	South Korea	0	1	2	3	1	41.3	194	40.8
2020	73			2	3	2	5	1	85.2	56	95.5
2020	74			2	1	1	5	1	36.5	227	56.3
2020	75			1	3	2	3	2	16.9	484	28.3

APPENDIX

Employer reputation rank	Faculty student score	Faculty student rank	Citations per faculty score	Citations per faculty rank	International faculty score	International faculty rank	International students score	International students rank	Overall score
160	45.8	325	54.6	185	29.1	471	31.5	415	40
501+	70.8	191	11	601+	15.1	601	49	296	32.3
68	41.9	365	59.7	144	20.8	540	30.4	427	67.3
316	64.2	221	43.6	291	24.3	508	36.7	374	37.6
202	9	601+	56.3	170	1.6	601	7.3	601	25.6
129	32.2	470	65.8	116	24.6	506	18	552	46.8
241	76.6	163	9.2	601+	3.7	601	5.4	601	28.2
14	88.3	89	75.7	71	100	23	76.4	158	91.8
501+	99.9	28	33.2	402	5.8	601	7.8	601	34.9
104	80.3	143	46.2	262	23.1	519	14.3	601	66.5
501+	96.4	55	36.2	375					29.2
12	72.3	182	73	79	70.7	248	36.9	372	84.3
233	99.9	27	99.3	9	35.3	423	3.6	601	62.6
30	28.6	524	13.6	601+	19.4	554	4.2	601	53.4
142	19.2	601+	1.7	601+	7	601	2.3	601	25
332	66.4	211	14.3	601+	100	11	98.3	51	35.8

Year	Code	Institution name	Country	Size	Focus	Research	Age	Status	Score	Academic reputation rank	Academic reputation score
2020	76	Seoul National University (SNU)	South Korea	2	3	2	4	2	96.9	30	91.1
2020	77	Shandong University	China	3	3	2	5	2	16.4	500	10.4
2020	78	Shanghai Jiao Tong University	China	3	3	2	5	2	79.6	66	93.6
2020	79	Shanghai University	China	3	2	2	3	2	25	331	6.4
2020	80			1	1	2	4	2	11.8	501+	23.7
2020	81	Singapore Management University	Singapore	1	0	1	2	2	14.5	501+	25.8
2020	82	Sogang University	South Korea	1	2	2	4	1	18.6	448	34.1
2020	83	South China University of Technology	China	3	2	2	4	2	12.1	501+	3.9
2020	84			1	3	1	3	2	12.1	501+	14.8
2020	85	Sun Yat-sen University	China	3	3	2	4	2	35.3	235	33.2
2020	86	Sungkyunkwan University	South Korea	2	3	2	5	1	58.4	126	74.6
2020	87	Taipei Medical University	Taiwan	1	1	2	4	1	9.6	501+	12.3
2020	88			2	3	2	5	2	28.4	299	34.7
2020	89			2	3	2	4	2	35.4	233	40.5
2020	90			1	2	1	5	1	24.6	344	37.4
2020	91	The Catholic University of Korea	South Korea	1	3	2	5	1	4.7	501+	1.9
2020	92	The Chinese University of Hong Kong (CUHK)	Hong Kong	2	3	2	4	2	87.9	51	61.5
2020	93	The Hong Kong Polytechnic University	Hong Kong	2	2	2	3	2	61.3	113	43.7
2020	94	The Hong Kong University of Science and Technology (HKUST)	Hong Kong	1	2	2	3	2	85	57	71.3
2020	95	The University of Tokyo	Japan	2	3	2	5	2	100	7	99.1
2020	96	Tianjin University	China	3	2	2	5	2	17.9	467	3.5
2020	97	Tohoku University	Japan	2	3	2	5	2	69.5	88	59.1

APPENDIX

Employer reputation rank	Faculty student score	Faculty student rank	Citations per faculty score	Citations per faculty rank	International faculty score	International faculty rank	International students score	International students rank	Overall score
45	88	92	61.6	137	19.2	557	11.9	601	79.6
501+	27.5	548	55.7	177	9.3	601	5.5	601	25.1
39	53.7	277	65.5	118	84.1	198	20.1	531	70.5
501+	54.9	269	17.6	595	46.3	349	5.2	601	27.8
394	14.2	601+	88.3	38	5.2	601	2	601	28
369	15.7	601+	24.3	488	100	35	67.8	195	24.9
282	51.9	293	13	601+	11.8	601	21	517	25.6
501+	21.2	601+	71.3	88	13.5	601	4.3	601	24.7
501+	74.5	167	11.2	601+	100	51	7.6	601	28.9
288	49.7	306	32.2	416	11.4	601	7.6	601	34.9
87	85.7	104	49.3	236	21.3	535	38.1	358	61
501+	87	98	21.6	533	22.1	521	18.8	544	28.9
276	24.6	584	69.5	96	64	275	3.8	601	37.2
235	7.8	601+	95.4	19	35.2	425	11.8	601	41.3
253	43.7	348	5.7	601+	93.9	141	3.8	601	28.4
501+	96.5	53	17.1	601+	3.2	601	4.3	601	25.2
121	67.7	204	56.2	171	100	52	91.7	101	75.9
213	74.1	173	46.3	261	100	50	74.8	165	61.9
94	59.5	242	89.5	33	100	16	87.5	120	80.6
16	93.3	69	67.9	102	11.1	601	26.2	469	84.3
501+	21.5	601+	71.6	86	9	601	6.2	601	27
130	98.2	42	43.1	299	12.7	601	17.6	558	63.7

Year	Code	Institution name	Country	Size	Focus	Research	Age	Status	Score	Academic reputation rank	Academic reputation score
2020	98	Tokyo Institute of Technology	Japan	1	2	2	5	2	74.5	75	82.7
2020	99	Tokyo Medical and Dental University	Japan	0	1	2	4	2	11.2	501+	5
2020	100	Tongji University	China	3	3	2	5	2	32.2	260	9.6
2020	101	Tsinghua University	China	3	3	2	5	2	97.4	26	99.1
2020	102	UCSI University	Malaysia	1	2	0	3	0	10	501+	35.1
2020	103			1	3	1	3	2	20.4	407	27.2
2020	104			3	3	2	5	2	71.6	81	90.8
2020	105			2	3	0	5	2	35.6	231	60.2
2020	106	Universitas Gadjah Mada	Indonesia	3	3	0	4	2	41.3	193	36.7
2020	107	Universiti Brunei Darussalam (UBD)	Brunei	0	2	2	3	2	13.4	501+	6.2
2020	108	Universiti Kebangsaan Malaysia (UKM)	Malaysia	2	3	2	3	2	50.9	153	44.7
2020	109	Universiti Malaya (UM)	Malaysia	2	3	2	5	2	68.2	91	72
2020	110	Universiti Putra Malaysia (UPM)	Malaysia	2	3	2	3	2	44.8	177	44.4
2020	111	Universiti Sains Malaysia (USM)	Malaysia	2	3	2	4	2	49.6	158	52.5
2020	112	Universiti Teknologi Brunei	Brunei	0	1	1	3	2	9.7	501+	9.8
2020	113	Universiti Teknologi Malaysia (UTM)	Malaysia	2	2	2	3	2	33.9	251	45
2020	114	Universiti Teknologi Petronas (Petronas)	Malaysia	1	0	2	2	1	12.6	501+	26.2
2020	115	University of Delhi	India	2	3	1	4	2	37.1	223	43.7
2020	116	University of Hong Kong (HKU)	Hong Kong	2	3	2	5	2	97.3	27	82.6
2020	117	University of Indonesia	Indonesia	3	3	1	5	2	39.5	205	47.3
2020	118	University of Macau	Macau	1	1	2	3	2	11.2	501+	6.4

APPENDIX 97

Employer reputation rank	Faculty student score	Faculty student rank	Citations per faculty score	Citations per faculty rank	International faculty score	International faculty rank	International students score	International students rank	Overall score
66	86.2	101	61.3	140	30.7	454	31.3	417	70.9
501+	100	11	21.8	527	3.6	601	16.7	572	30.5
501+	26.2	568	58.4	153	89.1	175	27.9	453	36.7
15	92.4	72	80.4	53	68	259	30.1	429	88.6
273	57.6	255	3.6	601+	41.7	384	81.1	142	26
345	58.1	252	11.8	601+	100	12	48.4	299	32.4
47	16.3	601+	14.5	601+	10.1	601+	8.4	601	45
125	13.1	601+	4.7	601+	8.2	601	2.2	601	24.4
262	51.3	297	1.6	601+	42.9	375	2.5	601	33.2
501+	94.9	61	6.2	601+	100	47	66.2	201	34.6
203	87.8	95	13.1	601+	24	510	38.9	351	48.3
92	90.7	78	41.5	317	62.8	280	57.2	251	67.1
204	73.2	178	20.9	541	58.8	300	82.3	135	48.4
158	74.9	165	17.7	594	37.5	411	46	309	47.9
501+	85.3	108	5.5	601+	99.2	77	16.9	570	28.9
201	73.3	177	22.7	511	27.3	479	53.7	271	41.4
358	35.5	441	20.9	540	82.2	208	30.1	430	24.6
212	12.1	601+	15.6	601+	1.7	601	1.8	601	25
67	87.2	97	44.5	283	100	22	99.1	38	83.8
186	43.4	353	1.9	601+	94.5	135	5	601	34.7
501+	24.3	586	43.9	287	100	10	96.2	72	28.7

Year	Code	Institution name	Country	Size	Focus	Research	Age	Status	Score	Academic reputation rank	Academic reputation score
2020	119	University of Science and Technology Beijing	China	2	2	2	4	2	19.2	431	5
2020	120	University of Science and Technology of China	China	2	2	2	4	2	56.2	132	26.1
2020	121	University of the Philippines	Philippines	3	3	0	5	2	34.2	242	39.5
2020	122	University of Tsukuba	Japan	2	3	2	3	2	35	238	13.1
2020	123	Waseda University	Japan	3	2	2	5	1	58.6	123	86.9
2020	124	Wuhan University	China	3	3	2	5	2	38	217	51.3
2020	125	Xiamen University	China	3	3	2	4	2	26.1	320	4
2020	126	Xi'an Jiaotong University	China	3	3	2	5	2	24.8	337	28.4
2020	127	Yokohama City University	Japan	0	2	2	5	2	6	501+	2.4
2020	128	Yonsei University	South Korea	2	3	2	5	1	62.9	104	78.3
2020	129	Zhejiang University	China	3	3	2	5	2	67.7	92	86.5
2013	1			2	2	0	4	2	39.3	317	35.6
2013	2			3	2	3	4	2	–	–	–
2013	3			1	2	1	4	1	33.3	380	69.5
2013	4			1	3	1	5	1	26.3	401+	79.2
2013	5			1	3	0	2	1	–	–	–
2013	6	Bandung Institute of Technology (ITB)	ID	2	2	1	4	2	–	–	–
2013	7	Beihang University	CN	2	2	2	4	2	–	–	–
2013	8	Beijing Normal University	CN	2	2	2	5	2	56.4	189	39.4
2013	9			2	3	1	3	2	32.0	401+	25.4
2013	10			1	2	2	3	1	–	–	–
2013	11			1	2	2	5	2	–	–	–
2013	12	Chiba University	JP	2	3	1	5	2	–	–	–
2013	13	Chulalongkorn University	TH	3	3	1	4	2	73.8	124	60.8

APPENDIX

Employer reputation rank	Faculty student score	Faculty student rank	Citations per faculty score	Citations per faculty rank	International faculty score	International faculty rank	International students score	International students rank	Overall score
501+	17	601+	65.6	117	4.5	601	4.1	601	25.2
362	81.1	140	98.5	14	16.9	588	5.7	601	62.3
240	62	234	2.1	601+	1.8	601	1.5	601	30.7
501+	70.3	193	22.3	519	16	600	30.4	428	36.3
57	32.2	470	7.9	601+	31.6	448	35.8	379	43.7
166	21.7	601+	46.5	259	50.7	332	10.7	601	37.2
501+	26.5	561	44.1	286	7.6	601	4.5	601	25.7
330	43.8	345	54	188	20.9	539	11.6	601	34.1
501+	99.9	25	10	601+	4.6	601	2.6	601	25.1
80	85	114	30.6	432	15.4	601	33.1	404	58.7
58	78.6	150	63.9	125	95.4	130	62.9	220	72.4
401+	91.3	79	1.1	401+	26.8	386	18.6	401+	40.2
–	76.6	137	1	401+	99.3	41	48.7	272	28.4
145	54.5	260	3.5	401+	97.4	51			36.9
109	66.9	177	20.3	401+	95.9	59	84.9	107	45.1
–	30.4	401+	8	401+	100.0	2	100.0	1	31.4
–	22.9	401+	2.4	401+			2.7	401+	29.2
–	83.0	121	10.9	401+	2.1	401+	6.1	401+	32.6
398	44.5	370	21	401+	72.1	184	28.6	401+	44.8
401+	56.8	240	33	369	79.6	155	14.3	401+	38.1
–	36.0	401+	15	401+	62.4	216	5.1	401+	31.0
–	26.4	401+	19.1	401+	28.9	371	23.4	401+	29.5
–	56.2	246	39.3	314	6.5	401+	16.2	401+	30.5
199	36.6	401+	10.2	401+	15.3	401+	3.7	401+	46.1

Year	Code	Institution name	Country	Size	Focus	Research	Age	Status	Score	Academic reputation rank	Academic reputation score
2013	14	City University of Hong Kong	HK	1	2	2	3	2	67.0	147	55.1
2013	15	Ewha Womans University	KR	2	3	1	5	1	30.9	401+	43.7
2013	16	Fudan University	CN	2	3	2	5	2	92.5	59	92.9
2013	17	Hankuk University of Foreign Studies	KR	2	2	0	4	1	–	–	–
2013	18	Hanyang University	KR	2	3	2	4	1	32.4	401+	50.2
2013	19	Harbin Institute of Technology	CN	3	1	2	4	2	–	–	–
2013	20			2	3	2	4	2	68.0	144	37.5
2013	21	Hiroshima University	JP	2	3	2	4	2	34.2	371	18.0
2013	22	Hokkaido University	JP	2	3	2	5	2	64.9	157	61.2
2013	23	Hong Kong Baptist University (HKBU)	HK	1	3	1	2	2	27.2	401+	25.9
2013	24	Indian Institute of Technology Bombay (IITB)	IN	1	2	2	4	2	58.9	183	89.2
2013	25	Indian Institute of Technology Delhi (IITD)	IN	1	2	2	4	2	51.3	215	86.8
2013	26	Indian Institute of Technology Kanpur (IITK)	IN	1	2	2	4	2	43.9	266	64.7
2013	27	Indian Institute of Technology Kharagpur (IITKGP)	IN	1	1	2	4	2	36.0	352	59.0
2013	28	Indian Institute of Technology Madras (IITM)	IN	1	2	2	4	2	40.3	306	74.6
2013	29	Indian Institute of Technology Roorkee (IITR)	IN	0	1	2	5	2	–	–	–
2013	30	Kaist – Korea Advanced Institute of Science and Technology	KR	1	2	2	3	2	85.1	79	72.8

APPENDIX

Employer reputation rank	Faculty student score	Faculty student rank	Citations per faculty score	Citations per faculty rank	International faculty score	International faculty rank	International students score	International students rank	Overall score
244	80.5	125	47.9	257	100.0	18	89.4	86	67.7
348	59.5	227	16.9	401+	23.2	401+	45.7	291	35.6
49	40.4	401+	64.9	142	18.3	401+	46.5	285	70.8
–	74.0	151	1.9	401+	54.3	243	36.2	357	31.3
290	96.0	53	15.6	401+	27.3	382	69.0	177	45.3
–	41.3	400	30.3	395			6.6	401+	28.5
401+	73.4	154	65.7	135	28.2	376	9.2	401+	60.9
401+	86.2	108	27.2	401+	8.8	401+	14.7	401+	39.5
194	88.0	94	45.3	277	13.5	401+	18.8	401+	60.6
401+	75.5	141	22.8	401+	87.5	113	74.8	148	41.4
65	28.1	401+	43	294	3.8	401+	1.2	401+	47.1
75	35.9	401+	63.3	157	1.3	401+	1.5	401+	49.4
177	25.6	401+	56.3	209	1.5	401+	1.2	401+	40.7
217	26.0	401+	57	205			1.0	401+	37.1
130	29.8	401+	46.6	266	2.1	401+	1.3	401+	39.2
–	33.3	401+	54.5	221					33.0
137	90.8	82	64.5	146	40.7	303	21.8	401+	75.8

Year	Code	Institution name	Country	Size	Focus	Research	Age	Status	Score	Academic reputation rank	Academic reputation score
2013	31	Keio University	JP	3	3	1	5	1	67.1	146	84.6
2013	32			3	3	1	3	2	38.2	331	29.2
2013	33			1	1	2	4	2	44.0	265	55.4
2013	34			3	3	1	4	2	43.3	271	35.2
2013	35	Kobe University	JP	2	3	1	4	2	39.3	319	40.7
2013	36	Korea University	KR	2	3	2	5	1	71.2	136	77.7
2013	37	Kyoto University	JP	2	3	2	5	2	99.9	17	92.1
2013	38	Kyung Hee University	KR	2	3	2	4	1	36.8	346	72.0
2013	39	Kyushu University	JP	2	3	2	5	2	66.8	149	75.2
2013	40			2	2	3	2	2	38.3	330	32.0
2013	41	Mahidol University	TH	2	3	1	4	2	47.8	241	29.2
2013	42			2	2	2	4	2	–	–	–
2013	43	Nagoya University	JP	2	3	2	5	2	72.3	133	64.7
2013	44	Nanjing University	CN	2	3	2	5	2	71.4	135	55.2
2013	45	Nankai University	CN	2	3	2	4	2	37.3	338	41.2
2013	46	Nanyang Technological University (NTU)	SG	2	2	2	2	2	92.4	60	94.1
2013	47	National Central University	TW	1	2	2	4	2	–	–	–
2013	48	National Cheng Kung University	TW	2	3	2	4	2	48.7	233	40.4
2013	49	National Chiao Tung University	TW	1	2	2	5	2	36.8	344	34.0
2013	50	National Sun Yat-Sen University	TW	1	2	2	3	2	–	–	–
2013	51	National Taiwan Normal University	TW	2	2	1	4	2	–	–	–

APPENDIX

Employer reputation rank	Faculty student score	Faculty student rank	Citations per faculty score	Citations per faculty rank	International faculty score	International faculty rank	International students score	International students rank	Overall score
88	60.8	215	19.9	401+	15.3	401+	8.2	401+	52.8
401+	53.2	271	2.7	401+	77.3	165	48.7	273	35.8
242	84.7	113	7.7	401+	100.0	12	61.6	201	49.9
401+	86.1	109	3.8	401+	96.4	56	17.8	401+	44.7
377	63.9	196	29.2	401+	8.7	401+	14.8	401+	39.7
116	79.9	127	27.3	401+	19.1	401+	32.0	386	60.5
53	94.8	59	68.4	124	16.5	401+	22.9	401+	84.1
139	83.6	116	11.5	401+	21.1	401+	47.6	279	44.5
128	98.0	43	29.5	400	17.8	401+	23.8	401+	62.0
401+	99.7	26	1.1	401+	15.7	401+	6.9	401+	40.0
401+	79.1	128	12.7	401+	14.3	401+	7.5	401+	41.6
–	21.6	401+	17.3	401+	8.0	401+	19.9	401+	30.6
176	94.1	65	57	206	21.8	401+	28.8	401+	68.4
243	41.1	401+	50.5	244	41.2	297	20.1	401+	55.7
371	46.5	345	28.4	401+	3.3	401+	24.0	401+	35.5
42	90.1	85	33	368	100.0	9	97.1	39	81.1
–	52.0	286	35	351	24.9	393	12.5	401+	33.1
385	47.9	326	47.9	259	20.8	401+	32.4	383	45.5
401+	59.5	225	62.1	162	51.3	252	47.2	281	47.5
–	25.0	401+	45.6	273	12.3	401+	8.2	401+	29.5
–	43.7	377	10	401+	18.1	401+	19.4	401+	28.7

Year	Code	Institution name	Country	Size	Focus	Research	Age	Status	Score	Academic reputation rank	Academic reputation score
2013	52	National Taiwan University (NTU)	TW	3	3	2	4	2	97.5	39	76.4
2013	53	National Taiwan University of Science and Technology	TW	1	1	2	3	2	–	–	–
2013	54	National Tsing Hua University	TW	1	2	2	4	2	59.6	180	40.0
2013	55	National University of Sciences and Technology (NUST) Islamabad	PK	1	2	1	2	2	–	–	–
2013	56	National University of Singapore (NUS)	SG	3	3	2	5	2	100.0	9	99.9
2013	57	National Yang Ming University	TW	0	3	2	3	2	17.3	401+	17.1
2013	58	Osaka University	JP	2	3	2	4	2	91.7	64	80.5
2013	59	Peking University	CN	2	3	2	5	2	99.8	19	98.8
2013	60	Pohang University of Science and Technology (POSTECH)	KR	0	1	2	3	1	51.7	212	54.7
2013	61			2	3	3	4	1	41.1	300	71.8
2013	62			2	3	1	5	1	85.5	77	87.4
2013	63	Pusan National University	KR	2	3	2	4	2	–	–	–
2013	64	Renmin (People's) University of China	CN	2	1	2	4	2	–	–	–
2013	65	Seoul National University (SNU)	KR	2	3	2	4	2	98.7	32	93.6
2013	66	Shanghai Jiao Tong University	CN	3	3	2	5	2	83.6	87	90.7
2013	67	Shanghai University	CN	3	2	2	2	2	–	–	–
2013	68	Sogang University	KR	1	2	2	4	1	–	–	–

APPENDIX 105

Employer reputation rank	Faculty student score	Faculty student rank	Citations per faculty score	Citations per faculty rank	International faculty score	International faculty rank	International students score	International students rank	Overall score
121	39.9	401+	77.4	95	17.5	401+	14.9	401+	**72.0**
–	59.5	226	22.4	401+	22.4	401+	23.9	401+	**32.5**
390	32.1	401+	76.1	100	41.3	296	13.3	401+	**52.4**
–	79.0	130	2.7	401+	5.2	401+	4.8	401+	**28.7**
16	89.1	90	57.3	204	100.0	15	96.6	44	**89.4**
401+	99.1	36	54.9	219	11.3	401+	11.3	401+	**40.7**
105	93.2	68	57.7	197	14.9	401+	19.9	401+	**76.9**
21	79.0	131	46.5	267	64.5	210	32.1	384	**80.0**
248	99.9	22	86.4	63	59.1	223	18.2	401+	**67.5**
140	65.6	185	1.2	401+			28.6	401+	**38.6**
72	42.1	393	17.5	401+	17.1	401+	21.2	401+	**57.0**
–	47.5	332	18.5	401+	12.4	401+	11.5	401+	**30.2**
–	48.1	323	3.8	401+	8.7	401+	16.7	401+	**29.6**
46	87.0	101	60.9	173	47.2	269	60.4	206	**84.1**
57	41.1	401+	54.9	218	20.4	401+	12.3	401+	**63.6**
–	30.7	401+	12.7	401+	6.9	401+	3.6	401+	**30.0**
–	62.6	201	10.7	401+	18.7	401+	26.9	401+	**32.7**

Year	Code	Institution name	Country	Size	Focus	Research	Age	Status	Score	Academic reputation rank	Academic reputation score
2013	69	Sun Yat-Sen University	CN	3	3	2	4	2	42.6	277	40.2
2013	70	Sungkyunkwan University	KR	2	3	2	5	1	56.5	188	87.4
2013	71	Taipei Medical University	TW	1	1	2	4	1	24.7	401+	32.3
2013	72			2	3	2	4	2	55.2	193	39.7
2013	73			2	3	2	4	2	59.6	179	40.7
2013	74	The Chinese University of Hong Kong (CUHK)	HK	2	3	2	4	2	94.5	50	83.3
2013	75	The Hong Kong Polytechnic University	HK	2	2	2	2	2	60.9	171	59.1
2013	76	The Hong Kong University of Science and Technology (HKUST)	HK	1	2	2	2	2	93.3	55	90.6
2013	77	The University of Tokyo	JP	2	3	2	5	2	100.0	7	99.3
2013	78	Tohoku University	JP	2	3	2	5	2	81.8	90	76.0
2013	79	Tokyo Institute of Technology	JP	1	2	2	5	2	79.8	101	84.6
2013	80	Tokyo Medical and Dental University	JP	0	1	2	4	2	12.9	401+	17.4
2013	81	Tokyo University of Science	JP	2	1	2	4	1	–	–	–
2013	82	Tongji University	CN	3	3	2	5	2	–	–	–
2013	83	Tsinghua University	CN	3	3	2	5	2	99.3	29	99.1
2013	84			2	3	0	3	2	–	–	–
2013	85										
2013	86			2	3	0	5	2	–	–	–
2013	87	Universiti Kebangsaan Malaysia (UKM)	MY	2	3	2	3	2	48.0	240	36.5
2013	88	Universiti Malaya (UM)	MY	2	3	2	5	2	58.8	184	60.8
2013	89	Universiti Sains Malaysia (USM)	MY	2	3	2	4	2	48.1	239	42.6

APPENDIX   107

Employer reputation rank	Faculty student score	Faculty student rank	Citations per faculty score	Citations per faculty rank	International faculty score	International faculty rank	International students score	International students rank	Overall score
388	29.0	401+	29.2	401+	13.5	401+	11.8	401+	34.1
71	88.3	93	26.4	401+	19.5	401+	38.0	345	57.4
401+	56.7	241	43.4	288	27.9	380	16.0	401+	35.5
394	38.4	401+	84.5	72	66.2	206	9.9	401+	54.6
379	14.4	401+	99.4	18	26.9	385	8.6	401+	52.6
91	87.9	95	47.1	265	95.8	61	81.7	114	82.3
216	46.7	341	41.2	303	99.6	40	89.1	90	57.5
60	86.5	103	52.6	233	100.0	10	98.6	27	84.4
18	91.4	78	76.3	99	11.1	401+	27.3	401+	85.7
125	97.9	46	54.9	217	18.5	401+	21.2	401+	73.1
86	76.8	136	78.3	92	15.0	401+	35.1	367	74.2
401+	100.0	12	68.6	120	7.0	401+	19.3	401+	42.1
–	5.5	401+	77.3	96			3.0	401+	30.5
–	38.4	401+	10.5	401+	3.4	401+	9.1	401+	28.8
20	88.6	92	38.3	323	48.7	263	38.9	340	79.7
–	35.2	401+	11.4	401+	100.0	4	86.1	102	31.7
108	19.1	401+	21.5	401+	12.2	401+	8.1	401+	49.3
–	16.0	401+	6.5	401+	11.9	401+	1.3	401+	29.3
401+	58.5	231	5.7	401+	93.0	84	44.6	296	42.7
200	90.0	86	7.5	401+	77.3	166	75.2	145	56.9
360	33.8	401+	13.2	401+	20.3	401+	39.3	337	36.0

Year	Code	Institution name	Country	Size	Focus	Research	Age	Status	Score	Academic reputation rank	Academic reputation score
2013	90	Universiti Teknologi Malaysia (UTM)	MY	2	2	2	5	2	32.2	401+	40.6
2013	91	University of Delhi	IN	3	3	1	4	2	–	–	–
2013	92	University of Hong Kong (HKU)	HK	2	3	2	5	2	99.4	28	93.1
2013	93	University of Indonesia	ID	3	3	0	5	2	48.8	232	67.4
2013	94	University of Science and Technology of China	CN	2	2	2	4	2	60.4	174	45.5
2013	95	University of the Philippines	PH	3	3	0	5	2	47.4	246	65.0
2013	96	University of Tsukuba	JP	2	3	2	3	2	52.3	209	36.0
2013	97	Waseda University	JP	3	2	2	5	1	72.3	132	85.4
2013	98	Wuhan University	CN	3	3	2	5	2	–	–	–
2013	99	Xi'an Jiaotong University	CN	2	3	2	5	2	27.6	401+	54.3
2013	100	Yonsei University	KR	2	3	2	5	1	76.3	112	82.0
2013	101	Zhejiang University	CN	3	3	2	5	2	72.6	128	72.9
2012	1			2	2	0	4	2	25.7	301+	20.4
2012	2			3	2	3	4	2	–	–	–
2012	3			1	2	1	4	1	30.3	301+	49.4
2012	4			1	3	1	5	1	25.8	301+	59.3
2012	5			1	3	0	2	1	–	–	–
2012	6	Ateneo de Manila University	PH	1	3	3	5	1	–	–	–
2012	7	Bandung Institute of Technology (ITB)	ID	2	2	0	4	2	–	–	–
2012	8	Beijing Institute of Technology	CN	2	1	2	4	2	–	–	–
2012	9	Beijing Normal University	CN	2	2	2	5	2	53.9	185	28.1

APPENDIX   109

Employer reputation rank	Faculty student score	Faculty student rank	Citations per faculty score	Citations per faculty rank	International faculty score	International faculty rank	International students score	International students rank	Overall score
380	62.2	203	3.2	401+	37.1	326	79.6	125	36.0
–	5.2	401+	4.8	401+			2.3	401+	30.3
48	94.7	60	51.7	239	100.0	19	98.7	26	88.6
157	56.3	243	1.5	401+	24.8	394	4.4	401+	39.4
327	60.3	219	70.9	115	12.7	401+	2.5	401+	55.9
172	39.9	401+	3	401+	2.3	401+	2.5	401+	34.4
401+	90.9	81	28	401+	15.7	401+	26.7	401+	50.6
81	35.4	401+	9.6	401+	34.1	337	24.7	401+	49.6
–	36.3	401+	14.3	401+			7.0	401+	32.6
254	72.9	156	14.6	401+	9.7	401+	9.5	401+	35.1
97	86.2	106	31	386	16.3	401+	37.4	351	65.1
135	30.0	401+	64.4	147	14.7	401+	20.4	401+	57.2
301+	84.4	92	1.1	301+	24.6	301+	14.9	301+	31.72
–	68.4	148	1	301+	97.5	46	46.8	255	
200	43.6	301+	3.2	301+	97.5	45			31.62
168	65.8	159	17.3	301+	88.6	98	89.7	71	42.21
–	28.7	301+	6.7	301+	100	1	100	1	
–	37.1	301+	1.3	301+	14.3	301+	10.1	301+	
–	22.8	301+	2.1	301+			2.8	301+	
–	42.7	301+	11.5	301+	8.3	301+	3.9	301+	
301+	47.4	275	16.7	301+	71	166	15.8	301+	41.96

Year	Code	Institution name	Country	Size	Focus	Research	Age	Status	Score	Academic reputation rank	Academic reputation score
2012	10			2	3	1	3	2	30.1	301+	8.6
2012	11			1	2	2	3	1	–	–	–
2012	12	Chang Gung University	TW	1	1	2	3	1	–	–	–
2012	13	Chiba University	JP	2	3	1	5	2	24.7	301+	9.4
2012	14	Chulalongkorn University	TH	3	3	1	4	2	79	88	66.3
2012	15	City University of Hong Kong	HK	1	2	2	3	2	73.2	115	42.8
2012	16	Ewha Womans University	KR	2	3	1	5	1	40.1	281	29.2
2012	17	Fudan University	CN	2	3	2	5	2	92.5	53	84.8
2012	18	Hankuk (Korea) University of Foreign Studies	KR	2	2	0	4	2	19.6	301+	70.3
2012	19	Hanyang University	KR	2	3	2	4	2	37.2	301+	31.2
2012	20	Harbin Institute of Technology	CN	2	1	2	4	1	–	–	–
2012	21	Hiroshima University	JP	2	3	2	4	1	36.5	301+	21.7
2012	22	Hokkaido University	JP	2	3	2	5	1	56.6	173	64.7
2012	23	Hong Kong Baptist University (HKBU)	HK	1	3	1	2	1	27	301+	36.1
2012	24	Huazhong University of Science and Technology	CN	3	3	2	4	1	–	–	–
2012	25	Indian Institute of Technology Bombay (IITB)	IN	1	2	2	4	2	59.5	158	82.7
2012	26	Indian Institute of Technology Delhi (IITD)	IN	1	2	2	4	2	53.4	187	79.4
2012	27	Indian Institute of Technology Kanpur (IITK)	IN	1	2	2	4	2	44.1	247	50.6
2012	28	Indian Institute of Technology Kharagpur (IITKGP)	IN	1	1	2	4	2	34.6	301+	42.3

APPENDIX   111

Employer reputation rank	Faculty student score	Faculty student rank	Citations per faculty score	Citations per faculty rank	International faculty score	International faculty rank	International students score	International students rank	Overall score
301+	47.6	272	31	301+	67.1	182	5.7	301+	32.59
–	42.6	301+	10.7	301+	60.7	191	5.3	301+	
–	46.3	288	67.9	121	3.8	301+	1.3	301+	
301+	66.1	157	32.6	301+	6.8	301+	18	301+	32.13
132	36.8	301+	8.4	301+	24	301+	2.8	301+	49.11
243	72.6	130	45.3	247	100	14	81.2	100	66.88
301+	50	250	14.3	301+	21.6	301+	33.8	301+	34.94
46	42.4	301+	51.4	209	18	301+	49.8	237	68.32
106	71	140	1.7	301+	51	232	36.2	301+	34.12
301+	88	80	13.7	301+	24.8	301+	49	243	42.46
–	51	245	25.6	301+			3.6	301+	
301+	82.4	99	27.4	301+	6.9	301+	16.1	301+	40.29
144	80.3	105	54.7	191	13.9	301+	18.1	301+	58.3
300	69.4	144	22.5	301+	88.4	99	65.2	171	40.88
–	63.2	171	9.9	301+	2.1	301+	3.5	301+	
55	28.9	301+	38.2	293	3.2	301+	1.2	301+	46.18
68	35.4	301+	54.1	195	1.3	301+	1.6	301+	47.83
194	28.2	301+	57.2	172	1.5	301+	1.1	301+	40.32
247	32.7	301+	47.1	238			1.1	301+	34.43

Year	Code	Institution name	Country	Size	Focus	Research	Age	Status	Score	Academic reputation rank	Academic reputation score
2012	29	Indian Institute of Technology Madras (IITM)	IN	1	2	2	4	2	40	283	73
2012	30	Indian Institute of Technology Roorkee (IITR)	IN	0	1	2	5	2	–	–	–
2012	31	International Islamic University Malaysia (IIUM)	MY	2	3	0	3	2	–	–	–
2012	32	KAIST – Korea Advanced Institute of Science and Technology	KR	1	2	2	3	2	85.1	68	51.7
2012	33	Keio University	JP	3	3	1	5	1	61.4	148	75.1
2012	34			3	3	0	3	2	38.6	297	19.8
2012	35			1	1	2	3	2	43.1	257	36.9
2012	36			3	3	1	4	2	56.7	172	22.6
2012	37	Kobe University	JP	2	3	1	4	2	38.2	300	43.6
2012	38	Korea University	KR	2	3	2	5	1	76.4	101	57.4
2012	39	Kyoto University	JP	2	3	2	5	2	99.8	18	81.1
2012	40	Kyung Hee University	KR	2	3	1	4	1	32.4	301+	60.1
2012	41	Kyushu University	JP	2	3	2	5	2	59.8	157	67.3
2012	42			2	2	3	2	2	24.3	301+	17.7
2012	43	Mahidol University	TH	2	3	1	4	2	48.6	216	21.9
2012	44			2	2	2	4	2	–	–	–
2012	45	Nagoya University	JP	2	3	2	5	2	69.5	128	64.2
2012	46	Nanjing University	CN	2	3	2	5	2	70.8	121	39.4
2012	47	Nankai University	CN	2	3	2	4	2	–	–	–
2012	48	Nanyang Technological University (NTU)	SG	2	2	2	2	2	90.4	59	84.5

APPENDIX

Employer reputation rank	Faculty student score	Faculty student rank	Citations per faculty score	Citations per faculty rank	International faculty score	International faculty rank	International students score	International students rank	Overall score
94	30.9	301+	40.3	279	2.1	301+	1.2	301+	38.09
–	37.7	301+	40.7	276					
–	38.2	301+	1.9	301+	56.6	206	81.3	99	
188	90	69	54	197	36.6	284	24.1	301+	71.77
84	59.7	188	17.5	301+	15	301+	7.7	301+	49.14
301+	57.1	203	1.7	301+	72.7	159	44.2	270	35.38
293	90	70	5.8	301+	100	8	56	201	48.38
301+	89.1	77	2.6	301+	93.3	69	19.8	301+	49.44
234	62.2	174	26.9	301+	8.9	301+	16.5	301+	39.13
172	70.4	141	22.3	301+	23.8	301+	34.7	301+	58.36
63	92.6	60	70	110	15.5	301+	21.9	301+	83.27
166	82.5	98	8.9	301+	19.2	301+	46.3	259	40.94
123	97.7	42	34.6	301+	15.3	301+	22.3	301+	59.59
301+	99.3	28	1	301+	15.3	301+	6.9	301+	32.99
301+	82	101	10.8	301+	12.9	301+	7.5	301+	41.63
–	23.3	301+	13.7	301+	8	301+	18.9	301+	
148	88	81	68.6	119	17.7	301+	29	301+	68.57
270	49.3	255	40.9	273	41.8	265	5.8	301+	53.22
–	36.5	301+	27.9	301+	4.6	301+	7.8	301+	
47	85.3	88	26.7	301+	100	7	97.9	29	77.69

Year	Code	Institution name	Country	Size	Focus	Research	Age	Status	Score	Academic reputation rank	Academic reputation score
2012	49	National Central University	TW	1	2	2	4	2	–	–	–
2012	50	National Cheng Kung University	TW	2	3	2	4	2	45.5	237	27.3
2012	51	National Chiao Tung University	TW	1	2	2	5	2	35.4	301+	23
2012	52	National Sun Yat-sen University	TW	1	2	2	3	2	–	–	–
2012	53	National Taiwan Normal University	TW	2	2	1	4	2	–	–	–
2012	54	National Taiwan University (NTU)	TW	3	3	2	4	2	97.3	38	70.3
2012	55	National Taiwan University of Science and Technology	TW	1	1	2	3	2	31.1	301+	22.6
2012	56	National Tsing Hua University	TW	1	2	2	4	2	58.1	163	27
2012	57	National University of Sciences and Technology (NUST) Islamabad	PK	1	2	1	2	2	–	–	–
2012	58	National University of Singapore (NUS)	SG	3	3	2	5	2	100	9	99.4
2012	59	National Yang Ming University	TW	0	3	2	3	2	17.1	301+	25.4
2012	60	Okayama University	JP	2	3	1	5	2	–	–	–
2012	61	Osaka University	JP	2	3	2	4	2	91.4	54	69.6
2012	62	Peking University	CN	2	3	2	5	2	99.7	19	96.6
2012	63	Pohang University of Science and Technology (POSTECH)	KR	0	1	2	3	1	57.5	166	37.4
2012	64			2	3	1	5	1	71.4	119	75.9
2012	65	Pusan National University	KR	2	3	1	4	2	–	–	–
2012	66	Renmin (People's) University of China	CN	2	1	1	4	2	–	–	–

APPENDIX

Employer reputation rank	Faculty student score	Faculty student rank	Citations per faculty score	Citations per faculty rank	International faculty score	International faculty rank	International students score	International students rank	Overall score
–	47.1	277	30	301+	21.2	301+	12.9	301+	
301+	42.6	301+	40.8	274	35.9	288	21.2	301+	40.88
301+	49.6	251	58.2	166	58.9	199	47.8	249	43.8
–	24.7	301+	40.5	278	16.4	301+	7.7	301+	
–	40.4	301+	8.7	301+	7.8	301+	18.2	301+	
107	38	301+	69.7	111	19.4	301+	15.1	301+	69.92
301+	54.9	215	18.1	301+	13.2	301+	22.1	301+	31.38
301+	30.8	301+	71.3	105	53.7	221	11.9	301+	50.15
–	75.6	120	2	301+	4.5	301+	4.4	301+	
14	81.4	102	51.1	212	100	13	98.2	24	87.24
301+	98.5	34	46.4	240	12.3	301+	11.4	301+	39.95
–	73.2	127	35.1	301+	8.2	301+	9.6	301+	
111	91.7	64	62.1	143	15.4	301+	20.3	301+	76.84
21	82.6	97	36.8	301+	55.7	214	35	301+	78.75
289	99.2	29	77.4	77	67.7	180	13.4	301+	66.79
81	42	301+	16.6	301+	17.8	301+	7.8	301+	49.65
–	44.4	301+	16	301+	12.2	301+	12.1	301+	
–	52.3	235	3	301+	8.9	301+	17.3	301+	

Year	Code	Institution name	Country	Size	Focus	Research	Age	Status	Score	Academic reputation rank	Academic reputation score
2012	67	Seoul National University (SNU)	KR	2	3	2	4	2	98.8	29	83.4
2012	68	Shanghai Jiao Tong University	CN	3	3	2	5	2	80	84	82.3
2012	69	Shanghai University	CN	3	2	2	2	2	–	–	–
2012	70	Sogang University	KR	1	1	2	4	1	33.3	301+	32.9
2012	71			2	3	0	3	2	–	–	–
2012	72	Sun Yat-sen University	CN	3	3	2	4	2	–	–	–
2012	73	Sungkyunkwan University	KR	2	3	2	5	1	55.1	181	53.7
2012	74	Taipei Medical University	TW	1	1	2	4	1	28.9	301+	23.5
2012	75			2	3	2	4	2	44.8	242	24.1
2012	76			2	3	2	4	2	51.4	203	24.9
2012	77	The Catholic University of Korea	KR	1	3	2	5	1	–	–	–
2012	78	The Chinese University of Hong Kong (CUHK)	HK	2	3	2	3	2	93.5	48	72.4
2012	79	The Hong Kong Polytechnic University	HK	2	2	2	2	2	60.9	150	39.2
2012	80	The Hong Kong University of Science and Technology (HKUST)	HK	1	2	2	2	2	92.5	52	79.7
2012	81	The University of Tokyo	JP	2	3	2	5	2	100	7	97.6
2012	82	Tohoku University	JP	2	3	2	5	2	76.4	100	66
2012	83	Tokyo Institute of Technology	JP	1	2	2	5	2	76.1	102	74.5
2012	84	Tokyo Medical and Dental University	JP	0	1	2	4	2	12.3	301+	6.6
2012	85	Tokyo Metropolitan University	JP	1	2	2	4	2	–	–	–
2012	86	Tokyo University of Agriculture and Technology	JP	1	1	2	4	2	–	–	–

APPENDIX

Employer reputation rank	Faculty student score	Faculty student rank	Citations per faculty score	Citations per faculty rank	International faculty score	International faculty rank	International students score	International students rank	Overall score
50	90.7	67	49.6	222	47.8	245	61	187	82.19
57	42.4	301+	43.3	258	20.6	301+	17.5	301+	59.88
–	34.9	301+	10.1	301+	6.4	301+	3.7	301+	
301+	53.6	225	8.7	301+	20.2	301+	24.7	301+	31.64
–	72	137	3.6	301+	98.8	34	3.3	301+	
–	24.9	301+	24.1	301+	15.1	301+	12.5	301+	
181	84.5	91	20.1	301+	18.9	301+	38.8	300	51.74
301+	47.9	269	50.1	219	30.5	301+	17.5	301+	36.28
301+	38.6	301+	78.5	74	49.3	240	6.8	301+	47.03
301+	14.5	301+	99.1	16	30.8	301+	8.2	301+	48.21
–	92.7	58	17.2	301+	4.5	301+	10.1	301+	
95	79.8	108	48.7	225	95.7	54	83.1	92	80.09
273	48.4	264	33.5	301+	99.9	26	88.2	75	54.62
67	83.9	93	54.7	192	100	12	98.9	22	83.48
18	89.3	74	73.1	99	11.1	301+	25.8	301+	84.95
136	96.8	46	54.4	193	22.3	301+	25.3	301+	70.5
90	79.8	107	70.8	107	14.3	301+	38	301+	71.35
301+	100	15	65.1	130	6.9	301+	19.7	301+	40.34
–	22.4	301+	67	123	10.2	301+	7.1	301+	
–	36.6	301+	41.3	270	12.7	301+	19.4	301+	

Year	Code	Institution name	Country	Size	Focus	Research	Age	Status	Score	Academic reputation rank	Academic reputation score
2012	87	Tokyo University of Science	JP	2	1	2	4	1	40.5	278	27.5
2012	88	Tongji University	CN	3	3	2	5	2	–	–	–
2012	89	Tsinghua University	CN	3	3	2	5	2	98.8	30	97.6
2012	90			2	3	0	3	2	29.1	301+	23.8
2012	91			3	3	1	5	2	75.1	104	66.1
2012	92			2	3	0	5	2	–	–	–
2012	93	Universitas Gadjah Mada	ID	3	3	3	4	2	–	–	–
2012	94	Universiti Kebangsaan Malaysia (UKM)	MY	2	3	1	3	2	48	223	26.6
2012	95	Universiti Malaya (UM)	MY	2	3	1	5	2	61.1	149	54.4
2012	96	Universiti Putra Malaysia (UPM)	MY	2	3	1	3	2	41.4	269	29.3
2012	97	Universiti Sains Malaysia (USM)	MY	2	3	1	4	2	52.5	193	29.7
2012	98	Universiti Teknologi Malaysia (UTM)	MY	2	2	2	5	2	34.1	301+	29.7
2012	99	University of Delhi	IN	3	3	1	4	2	–	–	–
2012	100	University of Hong Kong (HKU)	HK	2	3	2	5	2	99.3	24	83.8
2012	101	University of Indonesia	ID	3	3	0	5	2	52.8	191	64.4
2012	102	University of Science and Technology of China	CN	2	2	2	4	2	57.9	165	32.1
2012	103	University of the Philippines	PH	3	3	0	5	2	49.2	213	63.2
2012	104	University of Tsukuba	JP	2	3	2	3	2	50.1	207	22.3
2012	105	Waseda University	JP	3	2	0	5	1	73.9	109	78.8
2012	106	Wuhan University	CN	3	3	2	5	2	–	–	–
2012	107	Xiamen University	CN	3	3	1	4	2	–	–	–
2012	108	Xi'an Jiaotong University	CN	2	3	2	5	2	29.9	301+	40.6
2012	109	Yokohama City University	JP	0	2	2	5	2	–	–	–
2012	110	Yonsei University	KR	2	3	2	5	1	80	83	65.3

APPENDIX

Employer reputation rank	Faculty student score	Faculty student rank	Citations per faculty score	Citations per faculty rank	International faculty score	International faculty rank	International students score	International students rank	Overall score
301+	6.7	301+	77.6	76			2.5	301+	36.3
–	42.4	301+	7	301+	3.4	301+	9.6	301+	
17	86	86	32	301+	50.6	235	26.3	301+	77.51
301+	35.9	301+	10.4	301+	100	3	87	80	32.96
135	21	301+	20.7	301+	11.1	301+	6.3	301+	46.33
–	15.6	301+	5.9	301+	13.3	301+	1.4	301+	
–	22.6	301+	1.4	301+	23	301+	4.4	301+	
301+	57.6	200	4.2	301+	85.9	113	45.8	260	41.22
179	83.4	95	5.6	301+	77.4	145	70.2	150	55.62
301+	50.4	247	4.2	301+	17.4	301+	40	290	33.62
301+	28	301+	10	301+	26.3	301+	53.1	219	35.9
301+	58.7	196	2.5	301+	17.1	301+	72.1	140	33.65
–	3.9	301+	5.5	301+	1.3	301+			
49	94.2	54	50.5	215	100	18	99.1	21	87.89
146	54.2	220	1.5	301+	28.4	301+	4.2	301+	40.74
301+	56.3	209	61.5	147	9.3	301+	1.6	301+	50.99
152	37.3	301+	2.3	301+	1	301+	2.7	301+	34.45
301+	89.2	75	31.4	301+	14.6	301+	27.2	301+	48.98
70	34.5	301+	8.1	301+	32.5	301+	22.7	301+	49.22
–	28.6	301+	15.4	301+			7.5	301+	
–	31.7	301+	12.1	301+	10.2	301+	4.9	301+	
255	69.8	143	11.7	301+	6.9	301+	10.2	301+	33.52
–	96.6	47	27.3	301+	8.3	301+	8.8	301+	
140	83.7	94	25.5	301+	12.6	301+	38	301+	63.54

120 APPENDIX

Year	Code	Institution name	Country	Size	Focus	Research	Age	Status	Score	Academic reputation rank	Academic reputation score
2012	111	Zhejiang University	CN	3	3	2	5	2	70.5	125	59.5
2018	1			2	2	0	4	2	38.6	270	50.8
2018	2			1	2	1	4	1	31	353	49.3
2018	3			1	3	1	5	1	27	401+	83.7
2018	4			1	3	0	2	1	–	–	–
2018	5			0	2	0	3	2	–	–	–
2018	6	Bandung Institute of Technology (ITB)	Indonesia	2	2	1	4	2	52.9	182	56.1
2018	7	Beijing Institute of Technology	China	2	1	2	4	2	–	–	–
2018	8	Beijing Normal University	China	2	2	2	5	2	49.3	196	31.1
2018	9			2	3	2	3	2	27.1	401+	26.3
2018	10			1	2	2	3	1	–	–	–
2018	11			1	2	2	5	2	–	–	–
2018	12			3	3	1	5	2	–	–	–
2018	13	Chang Gung University	Taiwan	1	1	2	3	1	–	–	–
2018	14	Chulalongkorn University	Thailand	3	3	1	5	2	74.5	99	48.1
2018	15	City University of Hong Kong	Hong Kong	1	2	2	3	2	70.8	113	50.5
2018	16	Dongguk University	South Korea	2	3	1	5	1	–	–	–
2018	17	Ewha Womans University	South Korea	2	3	1	5	1	29.8	367	28.7
2018	18	Fudan University	China	2	3	2	5	2	91.4	57	97.1
2018	19	Gwangju Institute of Science And Technology (GIST)	South Korea	0	1	2	2	2	13.7	401+	5.5
2018	20	Hanyang University	South Korea	2	3	2	4	1	53.5	178	72.6
2018	21	Harbin Institute of Technology	China	2	1	2	4	2	26.3	401+	21.3
2018	22			2	3	2	4	2	55.6	170	36.4

Employer reputation rank	Faculty student score	Faculty student rank	Citations per faculty score	Citations per faculty rank	International faculty score	International faculty rank	International students score	International students rank	Overall score
167	29.5	301+	55.1	184	16.3	301+	6.9	301+	52.77
224	99	36	1.1	401+	30.9	395	14.9	401+	42.9
236	37.1	351	5.1	401+	90.7	140	5.8	401+	30.7
86	64.6	196	12.5	401+	99.2	60	68	192	43
–	20.3	401+	12.4	401+	100	2	100	4	29.5
–	69.7	168	2.6	401+	99.5	58	100	8	29.2
192	31	401+	2.9	401+	30.1	401+	2.6	401+	35.3
–	32.1	401+	36.2	354	6.8	401+	10.5	401+	27.5
401+	32	401+	44.5	281	33.3	382	14.7	401+	40.6
401+	20.6	401+	49.2	244	77.1	206	42.4	332	33.5
–	18	401+	26.2	401+	62.5	248	13.2	401+	29.1
–	5.6	401+	33	381	19.1	401+	16.5	401+	25.8
–	13.2	401+	2.7	401+	2.4	401+	7.1	401+	26.2
–	69	174	46.5	266	3.9	401+	8.3	401+	26.3
251	22.3	401+	8.9	401+	14.2	401+	2.7	401+	41.8
226	83.6	105	91.5	37	100	15	97.5	58	78.4
–	76.1	141	7.2	401+	12.4	401+	28.9	401+	26.6
401+	83.6	106	16.4	401+	10.2	401+	45.4	314	37.7
35	76.1	140	63.7	138	79.5	193	45.2	316	80.6
401+	37.6	343	100	3	11.5	401+	9.9	401+	34.7
121	76.3	139	29.7	401+	25.3	401+	38.8	364	53.2
401+	50.3	274	60	159	8.5	401+	7.4	401+	35.6
359	77	136	50.4	230	53.4	295	10.7	401+	54.7

Year	Code	Institution name	Country	Size	Focus	Research	Age	Status	Score	Academic reputation rank	Academic reputation score
2018	23	Hiroshima University	Japan	2	3	2	4	2	31.4	348	15.3
2018	24	Hitotsubashi University	Japan	1	0	1	5	2	–	–	–
2018	25	Hokkaido University	Japan	2	3	2	5	2	68.5	124	59.5
2018	26	Hong Kong Baptist University (HKBU)	Hong Kong	1	3	1	2	2	22	401+	18.5
2018	27	Huazhong University of Science and Technology	China	3	3	2	4	2	–	–	–
2018	28	Hufs – Hankuk (Korea) University of Foreign Studies	South Korea	2	2	0	4	1	18.7	401+	31.5
2018	29	Indian Institute of Science Bangalore	India	0	0	2	5	2	38.3	272	22.3
2018	30	Indian Institute of Technology Bombay (IITB)	India	1	2	2	4	2	62.3	149	77.9
2018	31	Indian Institute of Technology Delhi (IITD)	India	1	2	2	4	2	54.9	172	71.1
2018	32	Indian Institute of Technology Kanpur (IITK)	India	1	2	2	4	2	38.8	267	43.8
2018	33	Indian Institute of Technology Kharagpur (IITKGP)	India	1	1	2	4	2	31.4	347	49.5
2018	34	Indian Institute of Technology Madras (IITM)	India	1	2	2	4	2	41.1	252	51.6
2018	35	Indian Institute of Technology Roorkee (IITR)	India	1	1	2	5	2	–	–	–
2018	36	Jilin University	China	3	3	2	4	2	–	–	–
2018	37	Kaist – Korea Advanced Institute of Science and Technology	South Korea	1	2	2	3	2	89.4	61	87.4

APPENDIX   123

Employer reputation rank	Faculty student score	Faculty student rank	Citations per faculty score	Citations per faculty rank	International faculty score	International faculty rank	International students score	International students rank	Overall score
401+	83.8	104	17.5	401+	12	401+	15	401+	35.8
–	28.9	401+	6	401+	23.1	401+	27.5	401+	28.9
177	85	97	35.1	361	15.1	401+	14.2	401+	59
401+	35.6	367	52.6	210	100	50	86.3	120	37.7
–	18.1	401+	52	215	12.7	401+	8.1	401+	26.5
401+	78.3	127	2.1	401+	37.9	355	39	362	30.6
401+	56.1	244	100	6			2.1	401+	49
102	32.1	401+	50.8	226	3.7	401+	2	401+	49.7
125	15.3	401+	91.2	39	2	401+	2	401+	50.7
285	15.7	401+	73.2	98	2.1	401+	1.5	401+	37.9
232	12.9	401+	81.8	60	6.2	401+	1	401+	36.9
216	23.8	401+	67.6	123	3	401+	1.1	401+	40.2
–	14.1	401+	81.8	61	1.9	401+	2.1	401+	28.4
–	49	276	20.1	401+	16.7	401+	3.3	401+	25.6
70	70.1	167	99.5	11	25.2	401+	10	401+	80.4

Year	Code	Institution name	Country	Size	Focus	Research	Age	Status	Score	Academic reputation rank	Academic reputation score
2018	38			1	2	3	4	2	–	–	–
2018	39			1	1	1	4	2	–	–	–
2018	40	Keio University	Japan	3	3	2	5	1	63	143	80.2
2018	41			0	0	1	2	2	–	–	–
2018	42			3	3	2	4	2	31.1	352	26.9
2018	43			1	2	2	4	2	35.7	299	40.5
2018	44			3	3	0	2	2	–	–	–
2018	45			3	3	2	4	2	35.9	296	37.7
2018	46	Kobe University	Japan	2	3	2	4	2	33.8	314	36.8
2018	47			1	2	1	2	1	–	–	–
2018	48	Korea University	South Korea	2	3	2	5	1	76.8	90	88.1
2018	49	Kyoto University	Japan	2	3	2	5	2	99.7	18	94.9
2018	50	Kyung Hee University	South Korea	2	3	2	4	1	34.7	308	61.6
2018	51	Kyushu University	Japan	2	3	2	5	2	63.6	140	62
2018	52			2	1	1	2	2	23.9	401+	35.7
2018	53	Mahidol University	Thailand	2	3	1	4	2	46.4	215	24.6
2018	54			2	2	2	4	2	–	–	–
2018	55	Nagoya University	Japan	2	3	2	5	2	68.9	122	51.5
2018	56	Nanjing University	China	3	3	2	5	2	69.5	119	66.2
2018	57	Nankai University	China	2	3	2	4	2	32.6	329	18.2
2018	58	Nanyang Technological University (NTU)	Singapore	2	3	2	3	2	93.9	50	96.6

APPENDIX

Employer reputation rank	Faculty student score	Faculty student rank	Citations per faculty score	Citations per faculty rank	International faculty score	International faculty rank	International students score	International students rank	Overall score
–	92.6	67			19.5	401+	9.4	401+	25.3
–	97.1	50	1	401+	2.5	401+	3.5	401+	29.7
93	60.7	215	9.4	401+	11.9	401+	11.3	401+	48.5
–	69.3	172	14.2	401+	100	6	45.2	317	27.4
401+	67.5	180	15.8	401+	98.9	65	66	204	40.1
316	94.9	56	27.6	401+	100	24	46.6	311	50.3
–	77.4	133	1.4	401+	100	29	24.5	401+	26.6
345	89.3	79	13.2	401+	98.3	73	17.3	401+	44.5
353	61.8	211	15.2	401+	9	401+	9.7	401+	33.6
–	45.6	298	16.2	401+	42.6	340	10.5	401+	28.5
66	82.8	108	32.8	383	17.6	401+	36.7	379	65.5
47	95.7	54	56.4	185	13.1	401+	17.1	401+	81.5
162	71.4	160	21.1	401+	10.2	401+	28.3	401+	40.6
161	91.1	74	31.9	395	16.4	401+	19.9	401+	58.2
366	98.2	41	1.3	401+	31.7	389	5.7	401+	35
401+	58	235	7	401+	15.2	401+	5.6	401+	35.1
–	8.3	401+	23.2	401+	10.5	401+	8.8	401+	26.4
217	93.5	62	37	346	14.3	401+	20.5	401+	60.7
144	23.8	401+	85.3	50	69.7	224	18.4	401+	60.8
401+	30.1	401+	58.6	170	19.5	401+	8	401+	34
38	93.6	60	83.3	57	100	19	88.2	108	92.2

Year	Code	Institution name	Country	Size	Focus	Research	Age	Status	Score	Academic reputation rank	Academic reputation score
2018	59	National Central University	Taiwan	1	2	2	4	2	32.5	330	17.3
2018	60	National Cheng Kung University	Taiwan	2	2	2	4	2	49.9	194	42
2018	61	National Chiao Tung University	Taiwan	1	2	2	5	2	33.3	320	38.4
2018	62	National Sun Yat-Sen University	Taiwan	1	2	2	3	2	29.9	366	20.7
2018	63	National Taiwan Normal University	Taiwan	1	2	2	4	2	36.7	285	15.5
2018	64	National Taiwan University (NTU)	Taiwan	3	3	2	4	2	95.6	40	74.2
2018	65	National Taiwan University of Science and Technology	Taiwan	1	1	2	3	2	30.1	363	26.2
2018	66	National Tsing Hua University	Taiwan	2	2	2	4	2	56.4	167	50.8
2018	67	National University of Sciences and Technology (NUST) Islamabad	Pakistan	1	2	2	3	2	–	–	–
2018	68	National University of Singapore (NUS)	Singapore	3	3	2	5	2	100	11	99.9
2018	69	National Yang Ming University	Taiwan	0	3	2	3	2	14.8	401+	13.6
2018	70	Osaka University	Japan	2	3	2	4	2	88.5	63	75.4
2018	71	Peking University	China	3	3	2	5	2	99.8	14	99.9
2018	72	Pohang University of Science and Technology (POSTECH)	South Korea	0	1	2	3	1	50.9	190	65.6
2018	73			2	3	1	5	1	92.4	54	94.6
2018	74			2	1	0	5	1	–	–	–
2018	75	Pusan National University	South Korea	2	3	2	4	2	–	–	–

Employer reputation rank	Faculty student score	Faculty student rank	Citations per faculty score	Citations per faculty rank	International faculty score	International faculty rank	International students score	International students rank	Overall score
401+	31.7	401+	40.3	313	15.6	401+	19.6	401+	31
304	40.2	329	49.3	242	16.1	401+	26.7	401+	44.3
336	49.5	275	76.8	80	35.2	367	53.1	271	46.9
401+	27	401+	52.2	211	17.9	401+	8.2	401+	31.2
401+	73	155	11.9	401+	14.8	401+	86	122	38.3
116	33.3	392	74.1	93	14.5	401+	20.6	401+	69
401+	79.5	122	37.1	345	13.3	401+	28.5	401+	40.2
223	22.4	401+	90.2	42	24.9	401+	16.7	401+	52.4
–	74.6	149	6.4	401+	3.3	401+	4.5	401+	28.3
11	88.8	81	66.2	128	100	27	86.1	121	90.5
401+	99.8	28	37.4	343	5.7	401+	7.9	401+	35.5
112	71.9	158	63.1	142	21.5	401+	18.9	401+	72.1
12	66.6	183	61.7	153	52.8	300	48.5	298	80.8
148	99.5	31	99.8	10	42.4	342	6.2	401+	69.4
49	30.3	401+	11.4	401+	16.8	401+	5.6	401+	56
–	18.7	401+	1.8	401+	5.5	401+	3.9	401+	28.7
–	34.7	376	21.8	401+	8.1	401+	11.1	401+	25.2

Year	Code	Institution name	Country	Size	Focus	Research	Age	Status	Score	Academic reputation rank	Academic reputation score
2018	76			1	3	1	3	2	20.2	401+	20.7
2018	77	Renmin (People's) University of China	China	2	1	2	4	2	–	–	–
2018	78			0	1	2	2	1	–	–	–
2018	79	Seoul National University (SNU)	South Korea	2	3	2	4	2	98.9	30	97.4
2018	80	Shanghai Jiao Tong University	China	3	3	2	5	2	87	66	97.4
2018	81	Shanghai University	China	3	2	2	2	2	–	–	–
2018	82			1	1	2	4	2	–	–	–
2018	83	Singapore Management University	Singapore	1	0	1	2	2	–	–	–
2018	84	Sogang University	South Korea	1	2	2	4	1	–	–	–
2018	85			1	3	1	3	2	–	–	–
2018	86	Sun Yat-Sen University	China	3	3	2	4	2	42.4	238	49.4
2018	87	Taipei Medical University	Taiwan	1	1	2	4	1	15.5	401+	14.8
2018	88			2	3	2	4	2	49.1	198	45.5
2018	89	The Chinese University of Hong Kong (CUHK)	Hong Kong	2	3	2	4	2	94.3	46	83.3
2018	90	The Hong Kong Polytechnic University	Hong Kong	2	2	2	2	2	70.2	114	52.4
2018	91	The Hong Kong University of Science and Technology (HKUST)	Hong Kong	1	2	2	3	2	93	52	87.2
2018	92	The University of Tokyo	Japan	2	3	2	5	2	100	7	99.8
2018	93	Tianjin University	China	3	2	2	5	2	–	–	–
2018	94	Tohoku University	Japan	2	3	2	5	2	78.3	85	66
2018	95	Tokyo Institute of Technology	Japan	1	2	2	5	2	83.1	72	83.7
2018	96	Tokyo Medical and Dental University	Japan	0	1	2	4	2	14.9	401+	11.7

APPENDIX   129

Employer reputation rank	Faculty student score	Faculty student rank	Citations per faculty score	Citations per faculty rank	International faculty score	International faculty rank	International students score	International students rank	Overall score
401+	59.9	223	7.9	401+	100	10	99.9	24	33.8
–	33.9	388	5.9	401+	8.5	401+	7.5	401+	26
–	38.9	333	19.9	401+	48.4	315	21.1	401+	26.9
31	79.8	120	70.6	104	23	401+	16	401+	81.5
32	36.7	356	81.5	62	69.2	225	13.4	401+	72.5
–	38.6	336	16.1	401+	24.1	401+	3.3	401+	29
–	9.7	401+	84.3	51			1.3	401+	26.4
–	9.3	401+	21.3	401+	100	26	65.3	209	27.9
–	44.8	303	16.4	401+	11	401+	12.5	401+	27.8
–	62.3	208	9.6	401+	100	32	4.6	401+	27.3
235	28.6	401+	31	401+	30.6	398	9.9	401+	35.9
401+	84.7	100	18.7	401+	24.4	401+	17.3	401+	30.5
276	8.3	401+	96	26	29.7	401+	7.9	401+	47
87	66	188	50.7	228	99.8	53	84.9	126	78.8
213	58	234	54.5	198	100	45	80.2	148	65
71	54.9	256	87.7	47	100	17	93	87	84.3
14	92.6	68	73.3	97	9.7	401+	20.2	401+	84.8
–	30.6	401+	49.7	237	7.5	401+	4.2	401+	26.5
146	98.1	44	48.4	251	14.3	401+	18.1	401+	69
85	90.1	77	62.4	147	26.5	401+	24.4	401+	74.8
401+	100	7	23.9	401+	3.5	401+	14.1	401+	32.9

Year	Code	Institution name	Country	Size	Focus	Research	Age	Status	Score	Academic reputation rank	Academic reputation score
2018	97	Tongji University	China	3	3	2	5	2	36.1	293	27.5
2018	98	Tsinghua University	China	3	3	2	5	2	99.2	26	99.6
2018	99			1	3	1	3	2	19.5	401+	24.7
2018	100			3	3	1	5	2	82.7	74	85.1
2018	101			2	3	0	5	2	–	–	–
2018	102	Universitas Gadjah Mada	Indonesia	3	3	0	4	2	–	–	–
2018	103			1	3	0	5	1	–	–	–
2018	104	Universiti Kebangsaan Malaysia (UKM)	Malaysia	2	3	2	3	2	49.6	195	35.1
2018	105	Universiti Malaya (UM)	Malaysia	2	3	2	5	2	65.7	134	57.5
2018	106	Universiti Putra Malaysia (UPM)	Malaysia	2	3	2	3	2	49	199	34.4
2018	107	Universiti Sains Malaysia (USM)	Malaysia	2	3	2	3	2	48.2	205	43.8
2018	108	Universiti Teknologi Malaysia (UTM)	Malaysia	2	2	2	3	2	32.8	327	38.9
2018	109	University of Brunei Darussalam	Brunei	0	2	1	3	2	15.2	401+	1.9
2018	110	University of Delhi	India	2	3	1	4	2	–	–	–
2018	111	University of Hong Kong (HKU)	Hong Kong	2	3	2	5	2	99.1	27	93.4
2018	112	University of Indonesia	Indonesia	3	3	0	5	2	48.1	206	60.1
2018	113	University of Science and Technology of China	China	2	2	2	4	2	62.9	144	57.9
2018	114	University of the Philippines	Philippines	3	3	0	5	2	46	218	56.6
2018	115	University of Tsukuba	Japan	2	3	2	3	2	42.4	240	29.5
2018	116	Waseda University	Japan	3	2	2	5	1	69	120	89
2018	117	Wuhan University	China	3	3	2	5	2	43.9	226	57.9
2018	118	Xiamen University	China	3	3	2	4	2	–	–	–
2018	119	Xi'an Jiaotong University	China	3	3	2	5	2	29.1	375	27.6

APPENDIX

Employer reputation rank	Faculty student score	Faculty student rank	Citations per faculty score	Citations per faculty rank	International faculty score	International faculty rank	International students score	International students rank	Overall score
401+	24	401+	43.8	287	83.2	178	24.2	401+	36.2
16	86.7	86	75.3	87	42.1	344	25.6	401+	85.6
401+	47.9	283	11.7	401+	100	12	76.3	162	31.1
78	13	401+	12.8	401+	9.7	401+	9	401+	47.8
–	12.1	401+	4.2	401+	6.6	401+	1.4	401+	27.4
–	24	401+	1.5	401+	23.5	401+	2.4	401+	30.2
–	70.2	165	2.2	401+	59.9	265	9.3	401+	25.6
377	66.5	184	11.9	401+	44.7	330	39.9	356	43.4
184	87.8	82	24.3	401+	65.4	238	59.7	242	60.8
382	56	246	17.2	401+	43	339	73	174	43.6
284	46.7	288	22.1	401+	27.2	401+	27.5	401+	40.2
330	85.9	92	12.5	401+	35.2	368	51.4	277	41.1
401+	92.5	69	3.8	401+	100	47	64.7	210	33.8
–	7.8	401+	11.7	401+	2.7	401+	1.7	401+	26.1
52	85.3	95	46.3	271	100	18	99.4	32	85.5
175	44.3	304	1.6	401+	87.1	165	5.8	401+	39.2
183	67.6	179	96.7	23	14.4	401+	5.2	401+	64.9
191	40.7	327	2.1	401+	1.9	401+	1.5	401+	32.9
401+	70.7	164	23.8	401+	15.3	401+	32	401+	41.3
63	29.9	401+	7.6	401+	28.3	401+	34.2	389	47.2
182	22.8	401+	37.5	340	52.7	302	13.6	401+	38.8
–	24.8	401+	43.8	288	10.6	401+	8	401+	28.3
401+	48.5	278	38.5	332	28.9	401+	12.7	401+	34

Year	Code	Institution name	Country	Size	Focus	Research	Age	Status	Score	Academic reputation rank	Academic reputation score
2018	120	Zhejiang University	China	3	3	2	5	2	74	101	87.1
2019	1			2	2	1	4	2	33.4	245	48.9
2019	2			1	2	1	4	1	22.2	371	28.5
2019	3			1	3	2	5	1	21.1	387	59.6
2019	4			1	3	1	2	1	16.8	486	43.1
2019	5			1	1	2	4	2	4.9	501+	9.8
2019	6	Bandung Institute of Technology (ITB)	Indonesia	2	2	1	4	2	36.2	217	41.7
2019	7	Beihang University	China	2	2	2	4	2	16.1	501+	8.7
2019	8	Beijing Institute of Technology	China	2	1	2	4	2	21.2	386	7.6
2019	9	Beijing Normal University	China	2	2	2	5	2	37.8	204	14.8
2019	10			2	1	1	4	2	16.4	501+	30.8
2019	11			2	3	2	3	2	16.8	488	13.4
2019	12			1	2	2	3	1	20.5	395	38.8
2019	13	Chang Gung University	Taiwan	1	1	2	3	1	4.1	501+	5.1
2019	14	Chiba University	Japan	2	3	2	5	2	13	501+	5.6
2019	15	Chulalongkorn University	Thailand	3	3	1	5	2	58.6	118	44.9
2019	16	Chung-Ang University	South Korea	2	3	1	5	1	13.3	501+	21
2019	17	City University of Hong Kong	Hong Kong	1	2	2	3	2	55.6	129	39.2
2019	18	Dongguk University	South Korea	2	3	1	5	1	10.1	501+	11
2019	19	Ewha Womans University	South Korea	2	3	1	5	1	20.7	393	18.2
2019	20	Fudan University	China	3	3	2	5	2	81.8	61	95.9
2019	21	Gwangju Institute of Science and Technology (GIST)	South Korea	0	1	2	3	2	9.7	501+	4
2019	22	Hanyang University	South Korea	2	3	2	4	1	43.5	178	67.8

APPENDIX   133

Employer reputation rank	Faculty student score	Faculty student rank	Citations per faculty score	Citations per faculty rank	International faculty score	International faculty rank	International students score	International students rank	Overall score
72	37.2	349	80.2	67	54.2	290	25.9	401+	65.9
173	99.3	38	1.2	601+	34.4	426	23	487	41.3
346	47.2	326	5.3	601+	91.4	156	4.9	601+	27.1
126	67.3	214	14.3	601+	96.2	119	67.8	202	39
210	25.6	563	14.7	601+	100	2	100	4	29.2
501+	8.6	601+	92.7	28	4.2	601+	2.5	601+	23.6
219	43.9	353	3.2	601+	42.1	365	2.6	601+	30.4
501+	29.1	510	48.9	246	10.6	601+	7	601+	23.9
501+	32	477	44.1	290	6	601+	8.1	601+	25.2
501+	35.3	429	48.3	251	15.6	587	12.8	601+	34.8
316	95.3	61	1.7	601+	9	601+	24.4	471	30.8
501+	20.3	601+	52.7	205	72.6	237	26.5	457	27.7
237	21.4	601+	24.8	481	66.4	257	15.8	575	25.5
501+	72.5	184	47	267	4.9	601+	9.5	601+	26.8
501+	77.3	159	15.5	601+	9.3	601+	6.3	601+	25.2
197	28.1	529	8.7	601+	15.7	586	3.3	601+	36.3
448	80.3	148	10.4	601+	20.4	529	30.6	423	28.2
235	90.9	83	88.7	39	100	20	97.3	62	72.1
501+	85.2	117	8.3	601+	16.1	580	35.6	384	26.5
491	85.8	112	15.5	601+	10.6	601+	43.1	326	33.1
31	84.7	119	58.6	173	89.3	170	39.2	353	77.6
501+	39.8	389	100	3	9.9	601+	9	601+	33.3
103	78.6	155	30.6	421	27.6	470	37.3	370	49.4

Year	Code	Institution name	Country	Size	Focus	Research	Age	Status	Score	Academic reputation rank	Academic reputation score
2019	23	Harbin Institute of Technology	China	2	1	2	4	2	22.1	374	9.5
2019	24			2	3	2	5	2	40.1	189	31.9
2019	25	Hiroshima University	Japan	2	3	2	4	2	24.5	334	11.8
2019	26	Hitotsubashi University	Japan	1	0	1	5	2	21.5	382	63.9
2019	27	Hokkaido University	Japan	2	3	2	5	2	55.5	131	54.6
2019	28	Hong Kong Baptist University (HKBU)	Hong Kong	1	3	1	2	2	15.8	501+	14.3
2019	29	Huazhong University of Science And Technology	China	3	3	2	4	2	19.8	415	21.9
2019	30	Hufs – Hankuk (Korea) University of Foreign Studies	South Korea	2	2	1	4	1	12.6	501+	22.1
2019	31	Indian Institute of Science (IISC) Bangalore	India	0	0	2	5	2	35	227	16.3
2019	32	Indian Institute of Technology Bombay (IITB)	India	1	2	2	4	2	52.5	139	72.9
2019	33	Indian Institute of Technology Delhi (IITD)	India	1	2	2	4	2	46.8	162	65.5
2019	34	Indian Institute of Technology Guwahati (IITG)	India	1	2	2	2	2	13	501+	14.1
2019	35	Indian Institute of Technology Kanpur (IITK)	India	1	2	2	4	2	32.5	252	36.7
2019	36	Indian Institute of Technology Kharagpur (IITKGP)	India	1	1	2	4	2	26.5	314	44.3
2019	37	Indian Institute of Technology Madras (IITM)	India	1	2	2	4	2	35.2	224	45.9

APPENDIX

Employer reputation rank	Faculty student score	Faculty student rank	Citations per faculty score	Citations per faculty rank	International faculty score	International faculty rank	International students score	International students rank	Overall score
501+	56	281	65.8	123	10.2	601+	11.6	601+	**35.3**
295	81.8	139	46.8	270	67.1	255	13.8	601+	**49.1**
501+	84.1	122	17	594	12.7	601+	16.7	566	**32.8**
114	34.6	439	4.4	601+	25.2	487	26.8	456	**25.5**
148	87.2	107	33.3	382	19.5	541	14.6	601+	**53.6**
501+	40.5	379	52	214	100	53	89.7	107	**35.8**
434	17.9	601+	62.7	133	13.1	601+	7.9	601+	**27.4**
431	84	123	2.1	601+	42.9	362	40.8	342	**28.7**
501+	55.8	282	100	2	1.6	601+	2	601+	**47.1**
93	43.3	359	54.1	199	4.4	601+	1.8	601+	**48.2**
107	21	601+	84	53	3.1	601+	1.6	601+	**46.6**
501+	26.4	549	64.6	127	1.8	601+	1.6	601+	**25**
253	17.6	601+	75.6	77	2.1	601+	1.4	601+	**35.6**
202	18.3	601+	76.8	74	9.9	601+	1	601+	**34.7**
191	29.8	502	58.7	172	3.3	601+	1.6	601+	**36.7**

Year	Code	Institution name	Country	Size	Focus	Research	Age	Status	Score	Academic reputation rank	Academic reputation score
2019	38	Indian Institute of Technology Roorkee (IITR)	India	1	1	2	5	2	13.5	501+	21.6
2019	39	Jilin University	China	3	3	2	4	2	18	458	12
2019	40	Kaist – Korea advanced Institute of Science and Technology	South Korea	1	2	2	3	2	83.2	58	78.3
2019	41			0	2	0	4	2	7.4	501+	8.6
2019	42			1	1	1	4	2	11.9	501+	24.8
2019	43	Keio University	Japan	3	3	2	5	1	51.1	146	77
2019	44			0	0	2	2	2	6.4	501+	7.4
2019	45			3	3	2	4	2	24.9	330	25.1
2019	46			1	2	2	4	2	24.4	335	29.7
2019	47			3	3	0	2	2	6.2	501+	3.6
2019	48			3	3	2	4	2	25.1	327	27.6
2019	49	Kobe University	Japan	2	3	2	4	2	26.1	318	31.6
2019	50			1	2	2	3	1	16.3	501+	34.7
2019	51	Korea University	South Korea	2	3	2	5	1	66.7	91	84.7
2019	52	Kyoto University	Japan	2	3	2	5	2	98.6	22	93.2
2019	53	Kyung Hee University	South Korea	2	3	2	4	1	23.8	344	36.9
2019	54	Kyushu University	Japan	2	3	2	5	2	54.8	133	56.6
2019	55			2	1	1	2	2	13.2	501+	21.4

Employer reputation rank	Faculty student score	Faculty student rank	Citations per faculty score	Citations per faculty rank	International faculty score	International faculty rank	International students score	International students rank	Overall score
439	16.8	601+	89.5	36			2.6	601+	29
501+	52.3	291	23.3	503	20.6	525	3.3	601+	24.8
81	79.5	152	98.5	16	26.4	473	9.8	601+	78.7
501+	87.7	103	1.1	601+	37.4	400	16.8	564	24.4
393	87.3	105	1.2	601+	1.6	601+	2.1	601+	25.2
86	63.5	231	9.7	601+	13.4	601+	11.1	601+	44.1
501+	82.7	129	27.7	454	100	9	56.9	255	33.3
388	71.3	191	25.3	474	99.1	73	63.9	223	40
327	93.9	71	33.6	376	100	19	35.9	382	45.1
501+	81.9	137	1.5	601+	100	31	23.9	473	25.8
354	81.5	141	15.2	601+	96.2	118	11.8	601+	37.6
299	66.1	219	15.3	601+	10.7	601+	8.9	601+	30.9
274	47	330	18.8	574	44.2	351	6.7	601+	25.8
58	86.8	109	34.8	365	16.9	576	44.2	321	62.7
38	95.7	57	56.6	184	17.4	568	18.2	544	81.2
252	84.6	120	19.5	560	15.6	588	35.4	385	36.7
138	89.8	88	32.4	401	17.7	567	21.5	504	54.1
441	96.1	54	1.4	601+	24.5	492	5	601+	28.5

Year	Code	Institution name	Country	Size	Focus	Research	Age	Status	Score	Academic reputation rank	Academic reputation score
2019	56			2	2	0	4	2	8	501+	8.5
2019	57	Mahidol University	Thailand	2	3	2	4	2	35.1	226	23.3
2019	58	Nagoya University	Japan	2	3	2	5	2	60.9	110	45.7
2019	59	Nanjing University	China	3	3	2	5	2	58.5	119	41.2
2019	60	Nankai University	China	2	3	2	4	2	24.1	340	8.1
2019	61	Nanyang Technological University (NTU)	Singapore	2	3	2	3	2	90.3	38	92.6
2019	62	National Central University	Taiwan	1	2	2	4	2	22.2	369	15.4
2019	63	National Cheng Kung University	Taiwan	2	3	2	4	2	37.8	205	39.3
2019	64	National Chiao Tung University	Taiwan	1	2	2	5	2	26.7	312	37.1
2019	65	National Sun Yat-Sen University	Taiwan	1	2	2	3	2	23.4	350	17.9
2019	66	National Taiwan Normal University	Taiwan	1	2	2	4	2	26.3	316	11.8
2019	67	National Taiwan University (NTU)	Taiwan	3	3	2	4	2	88.6	43	70.7
2019	68	National Taiwan University of Science and Technology	Taiwan	1	1	2	3	2	23.4	353	23.5
2019	69	National Tsing Hua University	Taiwan	2	2	2	4	2	44.5	175	47
2019	70	National University of Sciences and Technology (NUST) Islamabad	Pakistan	1	2	2	3	2	15.9	501+	41.9
2019	71	National University of Singapore (NUS)	Singapore	3	3	2	5	2	99.8	11	99.1
2019	72	National Yang Ming University	Taiwan	0	3	2	3	2	14.5	501+	12.6
2019	73	Osaka University	Japan	2	3	2	4	2	79.4	63	70.5

Employer reputation rank	Faculty student score	Faculty student rank	Citations per faculty score	Citations per faculty rank	International faculty score	International faculty rank	International students score	International students rank	Overall score
501+	92.6	76	1	601+	21	518	12.6	601+	24.5
410	49.6	307	8.5	601+	15.1	594	5.5	601+	29.1
192	95.8	55	35.4	359	17.8	566	21	507	57.3
223	26.2	550	87.8	45	75.3	224	16.3	572	55
501+	33.9	446	61.8	146	31.1	444	8.8	601+	31.7
43	95	64	87.5	46	100	22	83.5	132	91.3
501+	34.8	437	38.8	337	21.6	510	21.5	503	27.4
233	44.2	350	45.2	277	17	575	29.4	435	39.4
248	52.3	292	68	111	38.5	390	43	328	42.6
500	30.6	496	46.9	269	18.4	556	8.6	601+	28.1
501+	78	157	10.9	601+	16.6	577	73.4	172	34.1
98	40.2	381	68.7	107	16.6	578	19.8	529	66.3
405	76.3	165	39.8	325	17.2	572	31.7	414	37.5
182	25.9	559	88.2	42	32.5	437	17.9	549	48
218	73.9	180	7.8	601+	3.5	601+	4	601+	27.3
18	91.8	79	72.8	87	100	24	80.7	144	92
501+	99.9	20	34.8	366	7.2	601+	7.5	601+	34.8
99	81.3	142	52.2	211	23.9	496	15.5	584	67.7

Year	Code	Institution name	Country	Size	Focus	Research	Age	Status	Score	Academic reputation rank	Academic reputation score
2019	74	Pakistan Institute of Engineering and Applied Sciences (PIEAS)	Pakistan	0	1	2	2	2	5.8	501+	7.3
2019	75	Peking University	China	3	3	2	5	2	99	16	99.8
2019	76	Pohang University of Science and Technology (POSTECH)	South Korea	0	1	2	3	1	38.7	199	49.2
2019	77			2	3	1	5	1	83	59	93.4
2019	78			1	3	1	3	2	13.9	501+	19.3
2019	79	Seoul National University (SNU)	South Korea	2	3	2	4	2	96.2	30	92.7
2019	80	Shanghai Jiao Tong University	China	3	3	2	5	2	77.8	69	96.1
2019	81	Shanghai University	China	3	2	2	2	2	25.9	322	8.7
2019	82			1	1	2	4	2	11.3	501+	16.5
2019	83	Singapore Management University	Singapore	1	0	1	2	2	12.7	501+	29
2019	84	Sogang University	South Korea	1	2	2	4	1	18.9	429	40.1
2019	85			1	3	1	3	2	9.5	501+	13
2019	86	Sun Yat-Sen University	China	3	3	2	4	2	35.4	222	44.4
2019	87	Sungkyunkwan University	South Korea	2	3	2	5	1	55	132	81.8
2019	88	Taipei Medical University	Taiwan	1	1	2	4	1	9.7	501+	13.2
2019	89			2	3	2	5	2	31.5	255	31.6
2019	90			2	3	2	4	2	34.3	233	33.5
2019	91	The Catholic University of Korea	South Korea	1	3	2	5	1	4.9	501+	2.5
2019	92	The Hong Kong Polytechnic University	Hong Kong	2	2	2	2	2	58	120	39.3
2019	93	The Hong Kong University of Science and Technology (HKUST)	Hong Kong	1	2	2	3	2	83.6	57	73

APPENDIX

Employer reputation rank	Faculty student score	Faculty student rank	Citations per faculty score	Citations per faculty rank	International faculty score	International faculty rank	International students score	International students rank	Overall score
501+	91.9	77	33.2	383			1.1	601+	28.2
10	64	229	69.4	103	68.2	251	53.8	268	82.6
170	99.8	30	99.6	10	46.6	343	5.4	601+	63
37	32.6	470	12.1	601+	20	537	5.1	601+	52.9
475	61.9	239	10.5	601+	100	12	99.5	34	32
41	87.7	102	66.5	120	22.1	506	14	601+	80.6
28	39.4	392	85	50	77.4	217	15.6	582	70.4
501+	51.6	296	16	601+	38.2	394	4.5	601+	27
501+	13.4	601+	86.7	48	1.9	601+	1.9	601+	26.5
338	13.8	601+	21.2	527	100	33	69.4	193	23.5
231	51.2	300	15.5	601+	13.6	601+	15.4	586	26.4
501+	65.4	223	11	601+	100	50	4.8	601+	25.7
201	41.8	370	30.9	417	19.1	548	9.3	601+	34.7
69	88.3	95	43.5	295	21.1	514	34	396	59.5
501+	93.6	73	18.7	575	28.5	462	20	525	30.2
298	24.4	579	70.6	96	61.5	282	9.9	601+	38.4
283	9.3	601+	95.9	21	35.3	414	6.7	601+	40.3
501+	96.9	51	17.4	587	3.9	601+	4.1	601+	25.5
234	65.2	224	49.2	241	99.6	64	78.6	155	59.1
91	61.8	241	89	38	100	15	87.9	114	80.5

Year	Code	Institution name	Country	Size	Focus	Research	Age	Status	Score	Academic reputation rank	Academic reputation score
2019	94	The University of Tokyo	Japan	2	3	2	5	2	100	7	99.5
2019	95	Tianjin University	China	3	2	2	5	2	17.2	476	6.2
2019	96	Tohoku University	Japan	2	3	2	5	2	68.7	85	61.8
2019	97	Tokyo Institute of Technology	Japan	1	2	2	5	2	74.6	73	80
2019	98	Tokyo Medical and Dental University	Japan	0	1	2	4	2	12.5	501+	6
2019	99	Tongji University	China	3	3	2	5	2	29.6	277	14.3
2019	100	Tsinghua University	China	3	3	2	5	2	97	27	99.4
2019	101	Ucsi University	Malaysia	1	2	0	3	0	6.5	501+	31
2019	102			1	3	1	3	2	17.2	477	22.7
2019	103			3	3	1	5	2	68.8	84	84.1
2019	104	Universitas Gadjah Mada	Indonesia	3	3	0	4	2	37.4	210	36
2019	105			1	3	0	5	1	7.7	501+	26.9
2019	106	Universiti Kebangsaan Malaysia (UKM)	Malaysia	2	3	2	3	2	47.4	160	33.6
2019	107	Universiti Malaya (UM)	Malaysia	2	3	2	5	2	63.9	99	57.7
2019	108	Universiti Putra Malaysia (UPM)	Malaysia	2	3	2	3	2	41	188	33.2
2019	109	Universiti Sains Malaysia (USM)	Malaysia	2	3	2	3	2	45.9	168	40.9
2019	110	Universiti Teknologi Brunei	Brunei	0	1	1	3	2	6.8	501+	9.3
2019	111	Universiti Teknologi Malaysia (UTM)	Malaysia	2	2	2	3	2	30.1	269	35.6
2019	112	University of Brunei Darussalam	Brunei	0	2	1	3	2	10	501+	3.7
2019	113	University of Delhi	India	2	3	1	4	2	34	236	48.5
2019	114	University of Hong Kong (HKU)	Hong Kong	2	3	2	5	2	96.7	28	83.7
2019	115	University of Indonesia	Indonesia	3	3	0	5	2	36.1	218	51.3
2019	116	University of Macau	Macau	1	1	2	3	2	10.9	501+	6.2

APPENDIX   143

Employer reputation rank	Faculty student score	Faculty student rank	Citations per faculty score	Citations per faculty rank	International faculty score	International faculty rank	International students score	International students rank	Overall score
13	94.2	70	72.2	90	12.3	601+	25.5	465	85.3
501+	26.2	552	62	143	10.3	601+	5.5	601+	26
121	98.4	46	45.7	274	14.5	601+	18.2	545	64.3
75	90.4	86	59.8	161	31	445	27.1	454	71
501+	100	9	21.6	520	3.5	601+	14.4	601+	30.9
501+	25.9	558	52.2	212	91.8	153	27.1	453	34.9
14	91.5	80	77.4	70	60.6	288	29.2	440	87.2
312	58.6	265	3	601+	50.3	328	75.4	168	24.4
419	57.6	270	11	601+	100	13	62.9	228	31.1
60	14.4	601+	13.6	601+	11.4	601+	8.3	601+	42.6
259	38.5	397	1.5	601+	36.5	406	2.6	601+	28.6
361	68.1	209	2.3	601+	62.2	277	10.2	601+	23.5
282	80.9	147	13.7	601+	44.1	352	38.4	358	45.5
135	93.5	74	32.6	399	55.9	311	61.2	237	62.6
285	67.3	213	19.7	555	55.9	312	74.4	170	43.8
225	64.3	228	19.6	556	36	411	37.5	367	43
501+	77.9	158	4.3	601+	98.8	77	20	527	26.1
267	85.3	116	17.1	593	27.8	467	58.8	251	40.5
501+	94.8	66	4.8	601+	100	51	65.7	214	32.7
177	11	601+	15.4	601+	6.4	601+	2	601+	24.2
63	88.1	96	47.1	264	100	21	99.4	36	84.3
163	49.1	310	1.8	601+	93.9	136	5.5	601+	34.8
501+	21.2	601+	34.6	368	100	10	96.7	67	26

Year	Code	Institution name	Country	Size	Focus	Research	Age	Status	Score	Academic reputation rank	Academic reputation score
2019	117	University of Science and Technology of China	China	2	2	2	4	2	53.7	135	35.9
2019	118	University of the Philippines	Philippines	3	3	0	5	2	30.9	260	49.6
2019	119	University of Tsukuba	Japan	2	3	2	3	2	34.9	228	18
2019	120	Waseda University	Japan	3	2	2	5	1	56.1	127	86
2019	121	Wuhan University	China	3	3	2	5	2	37.4	209	54.5
2019	122	Xiamen University	China	3	3	2	4	2	24	342	5.6
2019	123	Xi'an Jiaotong University	China	3	3	2	5	2	24	343	25.1
2019	124	Yokohama City University	Japan	0	2	2	5	2	6.3	501+	3.5
2019	125	Yonsei University	South Korea	2	3	2	5	1	59.8	114	81.6
2019	126	Zhejiang University	China	3	3	2	5	2	65.6	95	85

APPENDIX

Employer reputation rank	Faculty student score	Faculty student rank	Citations per faculty score	Citations per faculty rank	International faculty score	International faculty rank	International students score	International students rank	Overall score
262	74.2	178	98.4	17	15.9	583	5.9	601+	60.8
168	54.3	286	2.1	601+	1.9	601+	1.5	601+	28.8
495	69.3	203	23.8	495	18.2	560	33.7	398	37.1
54	33.1	460	8.2	601+	30.2	451	34.5	390	42.6
149	25.5	564	42.1	307	56.2	309	12.5	601+	37.5
501+	28.8	515	40.4	321	8.4	601+	5	601+	24.7
387	47.7	321	47	266	36.3	408	9.7	601+	33.4
501+	99.6	32	11	601+	5.2	601+	2.6	601+	25.4
71	86.1	111	33.4	380	17.2	571	38	363	58.9
56	60.9	248	69.2	105	86.9	183	45.1	313	67.5

Index

2020 QS World University Rankings report   7

academic peer-review   51
Academic Ranking of World Universities (ARWU)   6–8, 10
age   1–3, 14–17, 20, 29, 30, 32, 33, 36–47, 54, 86, 88, 90, 92, 94, 96, 98, 100, 102, 104, 106, 108, 110, 112, 114, 116, 118, 120, 122, 124, 126, 128, 130, 132, 134, 136, 138, 140, 142, 144
ASEAN   6, 13, 75–77
Asia   VII, 1–16, 20, 22, 29, 31–33, 35, 39, 47, 48, 51–61, 64–70, 74–84
Asian qualifications   9, 81
Asian region   1, 8, 10, 12, 51, 54, 81, 82
Asian society   82
Asian universities   3, 6, 7, 9, 10, 12, 29, 51–54, 57, 59, 67, 75–78, 80

Brunei   75, 96, 130, 142

Cambodia   75
capitalism   7, 66, 82, 83
China   6, 7, 10, 11, 75, 86, 88, 90, 92, 94, 96, 98, 100, 102, 104, 106, 108, 110, 112, 114, 116, 118, 120, 122, 124, 126, 128, 130, 132, 134, 136, 138, 140, 142, 144
China's Tsinghua University   6, 96, 106, 118, 130, 142
citation per faculty   14, 31, 35, 42
citation per faculty rank   14–16, 18, 19, 29, 30, 87, 89, 91, 93, 95, 97, 99, 101, 103, 105, 107, 109, 111, 113, 115, 117, 119, 121, 123, 125, 127, 129, 131, 133, 135, 137, 139, 141, 143, 145
colonialism   21, 82
corruption   12, 83
COVID-19 pandemic   68
culture   1, 8, 10, 11, 20, 21, 37, 57, 60, 64, 67–69, 74, 77–83
curriculum   4, 9, 37–39, 64, 65, 78–80, 84

development   2, 4–7, 12, 13, 20, 21, 31, 34, 37, 38, 47, 53, 54, 60, 64–69, 75–84
discrimination   21, 65, 69, 78

East Asia   5, 9, 53
eastern migration   79
editorial board   9, 21, 35, 60
education cost   5, 80
egalitarianism   66
elite universities   6, 9, 11, 19, 59, 60, 78, 80, 81, 83
elitism   68, 82
employment   37–39, 61
environmental issues   79

focus   VII, 1–3, 6, 8, 13–17, 21, 22, 29, 30, 32, 36–47, 51, 53, 56, 59, 66, 67, 70, 77, 80, 82, 83, 86, 88, 90, 92, 94, 96, 98, 100, 102, 104, 106, 108, 110, 112, 114, 116, 118, 120, 122, 124, 126, 128, 130, 132, 134, 136, 138, 140, 142, 144

Global North   VII, 7, 11, 20, 21, 82
global rankings   2, 6, 7, 9, 12, 13, 22, 29, 34, 52, 53, 57, 59, 65, 75–78, 83
Global South   VII, 3, 7, 9–11, 21, 56–58, 65, 67, 68, 79, 81
globalization   5, 10, 12, 20–22, 58, 60, 66, 69, 79, 80, 83
globalization of knowledge   20

Higher Education   VII, 1–15, 19–23, 28, 32–34, 39, 51–53, 55–60, 64–66, 68–70, 74–83
history   3, 10, 11, 17, 21, 36, 37, 50, 67, 68, 74, 78, 82
Hong Kong's University of Science and Technology   94, 106, 128, 140

indicator   1, 3, 8–13, 15, 17–19, 29, 31, 32, 34, 38, 42, 44–46, 51, 52, 54, 55, 59, 65, 66, 68, 74–81
Indonesia   75, 86, 96, 108, 118, 120, 130, 132, 142
inequality   7, 13, 23, 59, 61, 69, 70, 76, 80, 83
institutional characteristics   1, 3, 15, 17, 38, 40, 41, 45–47
institutional culture   57

INDEX   147

international faculty 10, 16, 17, 23, 29, 31, 35, 43, 44, 51, 87, 89, 91, 93, 95, 97, 99, 101, 103, 105, 107, 109, 111, 113, 115, 117, 119, 121, 123, 125, 127, 129, 131, 133, 135, 137, 139, 141, 143, 145
international faculty rank 1, 14, 16–19, 30, 44, 45, 87, 89, 91, 93, 95, 97, 99, 101, 103, 105, 107, 109, 111, 113, 115, 117, 119, 121, 123, 125, 127, 129, 131, 133, 135, 137, 139, 141, 143, 145
international student 1–3, 6, 11, 12, 14, 18–20, 29–31, 41–46, 51, 56, 57, 60, 76, 79, 82, 87, 89, 91, 93, 95, 97, 99, 101, 103, 105, 107, 109, 111, 113, 115, 117, 119, 121, 123, 125, 127, 129, 131, 133, 135, 137, 139, 141, 143, 145
international students rank 1, 14, 18, 19, 41, 42, 44, 87 89, 91, 93, 95, 97, 99, 101, 103, 105, 107, 109, 111, 113, 115, 117, 119, 121, 123, 125, 127, 129, 131, 133, 135, 137, 139, 141, 143, 145
internationalization 6, 15, 17, 19, 20, 41, 43, 44, 57, 58, 75, 76, 80, 81, 83

Japan 6, 57, 86, 88, 90, 92, 94, 96, 98, 100, 102, 104, 106, 108, 109, 110, 112, 114, 116, 118, 120, 122, 124, 126, 128, 130, 132, 134, 136, 138, 140, 142, 144

knowledge production 6, 7, 10, 21, 22, 53, 58, 64, 65, 67, 69, 75

language 10, 20, 21, 56, 60, 66, 67, 77
Laos 76
log of the overall score 18, 46, 47

Malaysia 76, 96, 106, 108, 112, 118, 130, 142
marketization and commercialization of knowledge 22
metrics 1–3, 15, 28, 29, 35, 36, 42, 43, 47, 48, 52, 57, 59, 81
minorities 11
modelling and analysis of QS ranking methodologies 29
Myanmar 76

national cultural identity 2, 4, 37, 65, 75, 82
National University of Singapore 6, 92, 104, 114, 126, 138
North-East Asian universities 75

Ordinary Least Squares (OLS) 1, 3, 15–18, 29, 38, 40, 41, 44–46

pairwise correlation 36, 37, 39, 42–44
  citations per faculty 42, 43
  employment rank 37
  faculty-student ranking 39
  international faculty score 43, 44
  institutions' academic reputation 36
Peking University 6, 92, 104, 114, 126, 140
Philippines 76, 81, 98, 108, 118, 130, 144
policy 2, 3, 7, 12, 13, 35, 37, 47, 51, 53, 54, 57, 58, 60, 66, 69, 77, 78, 83
politics 7, 12, 13, 19, 55, 60, 67–70
politics of scholarship 19
pollution 79
population of Asia 55
poverty 13, 69, 76, 80, 82, 83
power VII, 5, 7–12, 55–57, 60, 65, 67–69, 76, 81–83
private higher institutions 1, 5, 16, 19, 33, 34, 40, 44
public higher institutions 1, 5, 16, 19, 34, 40, 44
publication 6, 13, 17, 20–22, 29, 32, 35, 36, 37, 42, 44, 58, 60, 82

QS criteria 2–4, 48
QS World University Rankings data 6–8, 14, 28
Quacquarelli Symonds (QS) 1, 6, 7
quality assurance 55, 57, 77, 78
quantitative design 51

ranking criteria 1, 2, 8, 11, 20, 21, 31, 53, 55, 59, 60, 78
ranking methods 2, 3, 29, 35, 50, 53, 55–59
ranking scores 3, 46, 53–55, 57, 68, 79, 83
rape 78
region 1–4, 6, 8, 10, 12, 29, 31, 33, 34, 37, 51, 54–56, 58–60, 65, 67, 69, 76, 79, 81, 82
regression for institutional characteristics 15
regression of rank indicators 18
reputation VII, 1–3, 5–14, 16–23, 29, 30, 33–39, 41, 43–46, 51, 59, 74, 76, 78, 81, 86–145

reputation rankings   1–3, 5–14, 16, 17, 19–21, 23, 29, 35, 37, 41, 44, 46
research   1–4, 6, 9, 11–17, 20–23, 29, 30, 32–34, 36–47, 51, 52, 54, 58, 60, 66, 80–82, 84, 86, 88, 90, 92, 94, 96, 98, 100, 102, 104, 106, 108, 110, 112, 114, 116, 118, 120, 122, 124, 126, 128, 130, 132, 134, 136, 138, 140, 142, 144

Singapore   6, 7, 76, 90, 92, 94, 104, 114, 124, 126, 128, 138, 140
Singapore's Nanyang Technological University (NTU)   6, 90, 92, 102, 104, 112, 114, 124, 126, 138
size   1–3, 14–17, 29–32, 36–47, 76, 86, 88, 90, 92, 94, 96, 98, 100, 102, 104, 106, 108, 110, 112, 114, 116, 118, 120, 122, 124, 126, 128, 130, 132, 134, 136, 138, 140, 142, 144
social gap   80
social issues   1, 31, 34, 69, 74, 79, 80, 82
social justice   35, 47, 56
Southeast Asia   5–7, 12, 13, 55, 68, 75, 76, 79, 80
southern epistemologies   20, 21, 81
statistical analysis   12
status   1–3, 6, 8, 9, 11–17, 19–23, 29–31, 34, 36–47, 57, 59, 60, 69, 70, 77, 78, 81, 83, 86, 88, 90, 92, 94, 96, 98, 100, 102, 104, 106, 108, 110, 112, 114, 116, 118, 120, 122, 124, 126, 128, 130, 132, 134, 136, 138, 140, 142, 144

student mobility   2, 19, 21, 42, 56, 57, 68, 76, 82

technology   6, 20, 34, 68, 79, 80, 84, 86, 88, 90, 92, 94, 96, 98, 100, 102, 104, 106, 108, 110, 112, 114, 116, 118, 120, 122, 124, 126, 128, 130, 132, 134, 136, 138, 140, 142, 144
Thailand   76, 86, 90, 120, 124, 132, 138
Times Higher Education (THE)   6, 8

universities   VII, 1–23, 25–37, 39, 41, 50–69, 74–83, 86, 88, 90, 92, 94, 96, 98, 100, 102, 104, 106, 108, 110, 112, 114, 116, 118, 120, 122, 124, 126, 128, 130, 132, 134, 136, 138, 140, 142, 144
University of Hong Kong   6, 86, 94, 96, 100, 106, 108, 110, 116, 118, 120, 128, 130, 132, 140, 142
university rankings   VII, 1, 6–8, 12–14, 20, 23, 28, 32, 47, 51, 52, 58, 64, 65, 67, 75, 78–80

Vietnam   76
violence   78–80

weighting   2, 3, 10, 35, 43, 51, 55–57, 59, 81
West   2, 10, 11, 20–23, 57, 58, 60, 64–66, 76, 79, 82, 83
Western knowledge   77, 84
Western philosophies   78
world-class university   5, 6, 10, 12, 79
World University Rankings   1, 6–8, 12, 14, 23, 28, 32, 66

www.ingramcontent.com/pod-product-compliance
Lightning Source LLC
Chambersburg PA
CBHW061451300426
44114CB00014B/1939